KU-238-261

Contents

Introduction   4
How to use this book   15
Photo credits   96

▶ Short walks

walk 1: Cheriton
         3 miles (4.75km)   16

walk 2: West Meon
         4 miles (6.5km)   20

walk 3: Corhampton & Old
         Winchester Hill
         5 miles (8km)   24

walk 4: Buriton Village &
         Coulters Dean
         Nature Reserve
         4 miles (6.5km)   28

walk 5: Stansted Forest & Park
         3½ miles (5.5km)   32

walk 6: Kingley Vale
         Nature Reserve
         3¾ miles (6km)   36

walk 7: Cocking & Heyshott Down
         3¾ miles (6km)   40

walk 8: Burton Mill Pond &
         the Rother Valley
         3 miles (4.75km)   44

walk 9: Eartham Wood &
         Stane Street
         4½ miles (7.25km)   48

walk 10: Amberley Wild Brooks
         5 miles (8km)   52

walk 11: Rackham Banks
         5 miles (8km)   56

walk 12: Highdown Hill &
         Clapham Village
         4½ miles (7.25km)   60

walk 13: Chanctonbury Ring &
         Washington
         4½ miles (7.25km)   64

walk 14: Devil's Dyke,
         Fulking & Poynings
         4½ miles (7.25km)   68

walk 15: Clayton Windmills &
         Wolstonbury Hill
         4 miles (6.5km)   72

walk 16: Glynde & Mount Caburn
         2½ miles (4km)   76

walk 17: West Firle, Firle Beacon &
         Beddingham Hill
         5 miles (8km)   80

walk 18: Wilmington & Long Man
         3¾ miles (6km)   84

walk 19: Crowlink &
         The Seven Sisters
         3 miles (4.75km)   88

walk 20: Combe Hill & Jevington
         3 miles (4.75km)   92

Introduction

Fields near Cheriton

Walking in the South Downs

The South Downs are within easy driving or railway distance of many major towns and cities, such as Portsmouth, Brighton, or even the metropolis of Greater London. Even so, there are many quiet corners where rural peace and tranquility can be found where the only sounds to be heard are of insect or bird, farm dog or tractor, or simply the breezes rustling the treetops.

Walking is a pastime which can fulfil the needs of everyone. You can adapt it to suit your own preferences and it is one of the healthiest of activities. This guide is for those who just want to walk a few miles. It really doesn't take long to find yourself in some lovely countryside. All the walks are five miles or less so should easily be completed in under three hours. Walking can be anything from an individual pastime to a family stroll, or maybe a group of friends enjoying the fresh air and open spaces of our countryside. There is no need for walking to be competitive and, to get the most from a walk, it shouldn't be regarded simply as a means of covering a given distance in the shortest possible time.

None of the walks are especially arduous. The only strenuous sections are those that involve a climb up the scarp face from the valley to the top of the Downs. The grading given to each walk should be seen in this context. None are difficult to follow as all the routes follow public footpaths and bridleways – the only difficulty could be muddy underfoot conditions during or after wet weather. You should always be prepared for bad weather because so many of the walks provide little in the way of shelter. Always bear in mind that, on many occasions, you are walking across land on which someone depends for a livelihood, and every care should be taken to keep to official routes and to avoid causing unnecessary damage. It has to be left to the discretion of the individual whether to cross a ploughed field or to take a route around the edge. The Country Code should be adhered to at all times.

What are the South Downs?

The natural world represents only a part of the story of the Downs, for the landscape we see today would look very different if people had not intervened. The Neolithic Age which lasted from around 4000 to 2000BC saw the development of the flint as a cutting tool which was used to clear the trees from the upland Downs. More specific features have been left behind. The most obvious are the long barrows or burial mounds, which each might once have contained as many as fifty bodies. A fine example is to be seen on Cissbury Hill.

The people of the Iron Age of around 500BC used ploughs that coped with the thin soil of the uplands and worked small fields on the hillsides. With repeated ploughings the soil piled up on the downhill side in distinct ridges, and, because the fields were often set at odd angles, these ridges formed on all four sides. They are known as 'lynchers', examples of which can be seen on the hillside above Jevington. It is from this period up until Roman times that some of the most striking and distinctive of the downland features were built – hill forts.

The Celtic tribes who built the hill forts and ploughed the Downs were eventually to be defeated by the invading armies of Rome. The most obvious Roman relic is Stane Street which ran from Chichester to London – it is followed by the walk through Eartham Wood. Close to Stane Street are the very impressive remains of the Roman villa at Bignor, which is open to the public.

The end of the 5th century saw the arrival of Christianity and the conversion of the Saxons, who had settled in Sussex. A few churches from this period still survive, the siting of which represent a vital shift in emphasis. The hill forts of the Iron Age had given way to the villages of the valleys and the Weald. Villages were established at regular intervals all along the foot of the north-facing escarpment, taking advantage of the freshwater springs that flow out from the chalk. These provided drinking water and also as a means of washing the downland sheep, so that their fleeces were ready for market. These springs are seen at their clearest at Fulking, where they flow out through elaborate ceramic surrounds.

These rivers formed the main highways of trade for many hundreds of years, as river transport was cheaper than movement overland and the heavy clays of the Weald made tracks all but impassable in wet seasons before the advent of surfaced roads. The rivers snake inland through the hills, and the end of the tideway is often marked by an important development. Towns such as Arundel and Lewes owe their importance to their roles as links between the interior of south-east England and the sea. Arundel is centred on the great castle that guards the point where the River Arun breaks through the hills to make its way to the sea. Modern developments have now reduced the town to the status of a picturesque backwater but at one time it had a busy wharf area and a brisk trade, with canal connections with London. It is this importance of river communication that created all the major towns that one meets throughout the whole region.

Even the smaller towns, higher up the minor rivers, profited from their maritime connections. Alfriston on the Cuckmere grew rich on European trade, both licit and illicit, for it was a notorious haunt of smugglers.

The origin of the most historic of the buildings are as a result of stone not being available locally, so builders turned to other materials, the most obvious of which is timber. The timberframed houses were built as a jigsaw of horizontal and vertical members, all cut to size and then assembled on site. All that was needed after that was a suitable material to plug the gap – wattle and daub in the oldest buildings, bricks in the more recent. The clays of the Weald are ideal for manufacturing bricks and tiles. A thatched or tiled roof produced a simple picturesque home. Designers of more important structures, such as churches, were faced with the dilemma of either importing building stone at great expense or finding a local alternative such as flint which was embedded in plaster to create a wall.

What we now see as colourful, picturesque villages turn out to be no more than local responses to local needs. Perhaps it is here that their charm lies, for the villages and towns belong to this particular region of England and to no other.

Geology and Landscape

The landscape of the Downs has been formed over a period that stretches back over millions of years. This whole region was covered by a vast, freshwater lake, the bed of which was made up of sands and clays. When the sea broke through, myriads of tiny shellfish were brought with it. When they died, their bodies sank to the seabed where they decomposed leaving their hard skeletons behind, forming the white mass we know as chalk. Eventually, the sea receded, leaving a land where a layer of chalk sat above the soft sands and clays. A period of great upheaval followed and the landmass buckled to form hills and ridges, valleys and depressions.

A great dome was formed stretching all the way from what is now southern England to France. In time, the sea swept through to form the English Channel, leaving just part of this dome behind in England. Subsequently, the slow, inexorable forces of wind and rain began to eat into the chalk. The centre of the dome was destroyed, leaving the rest as two ridges with a deep depression between. This, in effect, is the landscape we see today: the two chalk ridges of the North and South Downs, separated by the plain of the Weald.

The rolling undulating landscape of the Downs is produced by the gentle weathering of the chalk. The steep, scarp face that marks the northern edge of the South Downs is simply the result of the collapse of the central portion of the once-extensive dome. The rivers that have forced their way through the ridge have created their own landscape of flat, marshy flood plains while, in the central, eroded area of the Weald, the weather has cut right through to expose ancient sands and clays. So, in walking the Weald you often find the paths are heavy and often soggy. In contrast, on the uplands, the chalk has been exposed which provides a firm, sparkling-white path in dry weather but which can become a grey slither in the wet.

The differences between the uplands of the chalk downs, and the clay lowlands of the Weald are substantial. The former has a landscape of thin soil, which can only be made to support crops with a great deal of difficulty. At the eastern end of the Downs, the overlying soil is at its thinnest – just how thin that cover is can be seen where the sea has broken through to create the tall, white cliffs of the Seven Sisters. Here, trees are, at best, poor stunted things so there is little cover from the sun or rain. Down in the Weald, things are very different, for the clays once supported a vast area of forest, traces of which remain in isolated copses and more extensive areas of woodland. There is plenty of shelter but the heavy soil can make it hard going in the wet and, where individual walks are indicated as being difficult in wet weather, the warnings should be taken seriously.

Wildlife in the South Downs
The different habitats of the area all have their own characteristic plants and animals. Modern, mechanised farming techniques and intensive use of fertilisers have brought much of the area of the upland Downs under cultivation. This has resulted in a dearth of wild flowers and plants in those regions. But the phenomenon is not new. The Downs used to be covered by rough woodland and scrub that had to be cleared before cultivation could begin. During the Stone Age, the downland was cultivated, simply because the thin soil provided less of an obstacle to the primitive ploughs than did the heavy clays of the Weald.

Countryside near West Firle

The thin, chalky soils of the uncultivated Downs have their own quite distinctive plant life, which give the special character to virtually all the walks in this book. There are three principal grasses that make up the turf: sheep's fescue, the tall, upright brome, and carnation sedge with its distinctive bluish-green leaves. Herbs thrive among the grasses, lending their scents to the hill air: salad burnet is common, and you can find such plants as selfheal, which was once used for treating cuts and wounds. There are many small flowers that thrive, such as milkwort, which can be blue, white, or pink, the brilliant yellow bird's-foot trefoil, and vetches. However, the true glory of the Downs are the orchids which can still be found over wide areas of uncultivated land. The plants provide the attraction for a rich insect life and, in summer, butterflies are common, particularly the small heath and the beautiful chalkhill blue.

The song of the skylark forms what can seem an almost continuous, and always beautiful, accompaniment to any walk on the uplands. The corn bunting, partridge, and quail offer rather less musical accompaniment, and the cuckoo regularly joins in the chorus. A common sight, hovering over the Downs, is the kestrel. The more heavily wooded sections to the west have their own inhabitants, such as the treecreeper and the nuthatch, while the staccato rattle of the woodpecker often echoes through the trees. Of the remaining animal life, the rabbit is by far the commonest, but deer can also be seen, albeit briefly, at the edges of woods. Adders live in the downs, but should not be a cause for concern – they are as keen to avoid contact with walkers, as walkers are anxious to avoid them. The harmless slowworm is also occasionally seen.

Elsewhere, there are meadows of buttercups, daisies and dandelions, fields of brilliant red poppies stretched out at the foot of the Downs as well as woodland dominated by beech and oak trees. Bushes frequently drip with travellers'-joy which, in autumn, hangs down in the grey feathery fronds that earn it the alternative name of old-man's beard. The commonest bird cries are those of the woodpigeon while the river valleys can boast a fine mixture of waterfowl and seabirds straying upriver from the coast.

Kingley Vale

South Downs National Park

The South Downs National Park was first proposed in 1947 but not officially recognised until 2010 and covers 636 square miles (1648 sq. km) from St Catherine's Hill, near Winchester in the west to Beachy Head in the east. It encompasses two former Areas Of Outstanding Natural Beauty – East Hampshire and the Sussex Downs – and runs across the counties of Hampshire, East and West Sussex

It was also in 1947 that a Special Committee on Footpaths and Access to the Countryside recommended the establishment of six long-distance footpaths, the South Downs Way among them. The route was not, however, officially opened until 1972 but it is now established as a popular, well-used route for walkers and many of the walks in this guide make use of it. Leisure is the latest of the many changes that have overtaken the countryside, the designation of the National Park being the final piece in the jigsaw.

Walking tips & guidance

Safety

As with all other outdoor activities, walking is safe provided a few simple commonsense rules are followed:

- Make sure you are fit enough to complete the walk;

- Always try to let others know where you intend going, especially if you are walking alone;

- Be clothed adequately for the weather and always wear suitable footwear;

- Always allow plenty of time for the walk, especially if it is longer or harder than you have done before;

- Whatever the distance you plan to walk, always allow plenty of daylight hours unless you are absolutely certain of the route;

- If mist or bad weather come on unexpectedly, do not panic but instead try to remember the last certain feature which you have passed (road, farm, wood, etc.). Then work out your route from that point on the map but be sure of your route before continuing;

- Do not dislodge stones on the high edges: there may be climbers or other walkers on the lower crags and slopes;

- Unfortunately, accidents can happen even on the easiest of walks. If this should be the case and you need the help of others, make sure that the injured person is safe in a place where no further injury is likely to occur. For example, the injured person should not be left on a steep hillside or in danger from falling rocks. If you have a mobile phone and there is a signal, call for assistance. If, however, you are unable to contact help by mobile and you cannot leave anyone with the injured person, and even if they are conscious, try to leave a written note explaining their injuries and whatever you have done in the way of first aid treatment. Make sure you know exactly where you left them and then go to find assistance. Make your way to a telephone, dial 999 and ask for the police or mountain rescue. Unless the accident has happened within easy access of a road, it is the responsibility of the police to arrange evacuation. Always give accurate directions on how to find the casualty and, if possible, give an indication of the injuries involved;

- When walking in open country, learn to keep an eye on the immediate foreground while you admire the scenery or plan the route ahead. This may sound difficult but will enhance your walking experience;

- It's best to walk at a steady pace, always on the flat of the feet as this is less tiring. Try not to walk directly up or downhill. A zigzag route is a more comfortable way of negotiating a slope. Running directly downhill is a major cause of erosion on popular hillsides;

- When walking along a country road, walk on the right, facing the traffic. The exception to this rule is, when approaching a blind bend, the walker should cross over to the left and so have a clear view and also be seen in both directions;

- Finally, always park your car where it will not cause inconvenience to other road users or prevent a farmer from gaining access to his fields. Take any valuables with you or lock them out of sight in the car.

Equipment

Equipment, including clothing, footwear and rucksacks, is essentially a personal thing and depends on several factors, such as the type of activity planned, the time of year, and weather likely to be encountered.

All too often, a novice walker will spend money on a fashionable jacket but will skimp when it comes to buying footwear or a comfortable rucksack. Blistered and tired feet quickly remove all enjoyment from even the most exciting walk and a poorly balanced rucksack will soon feel as though you are carrying a ton of bricks. Well designed equipment is not only more comfortable but, being better made, it is longer lasting.

Clothing should be adequate for the day. In summer, remember to protect your head and neck, which are particularly vulnerable in a strong sun and use sun screen. Wear light woollen socks and lightweight boots or strong shoes. A spare pullover and waterproofs carried in the rucksack should, however, always be there in case you need them.

Winter wear is a much more serious affair. Remember that once the body starts to lose heat, it becomes much less efficient. Jeans are particularly unsuitable for winter wear and can sometimes even be downright dangerous.

Waterproof clothing is an area where it pays to buy the best you can afford. Make sure that the jacket is loose-fitting, windproof and has a generous hood. Waterproof overtrousers will not only offer complete protection in the rain but they are also windproof. Do not be misled by flimsy nylon 'showerproof' items. Remember, too, that garments made from rubberised or plastic material are heavy to carry and wear and they trap body condensation. Your rucksack should have wide, padded carrying straps for comfort.

It is important to wear boots that fit well or shoes with a good moulded sole – blisters can ruin any walk! Woollen socks are much more comfortable than any other fibre. Your clothes should be comfortable and not likely to catch on twigs and bushes.

It is important to carry a compass, preferably one of the 'Silva' type as well as this guide. A smaller scale map covering a wider area can add to the enjoyment of a walk. Binoculars are not essential but are very useful for spotting distant stiles and give added interest to viewpoints and wildlife. Although none of the walks in this guide venture too far from civilisation, on a hot day even the shortest of walks can lead to dehydration so a bottle of water is advisable.

Finally, a small first aid kit is an invaluable help in coping with cuts and other small injuries.

Public Rights of Way

In 1949, the National Parks and Access to the Countryside Act tidied up the law covering rights of way. Following public consultation, maps were drawn up by the Countryside Authorities of England and Wales to show all the rights of way. Copies of these maps are available for public inspection and are invaluable when trying to resolve doubts over little-used footpaths. Once on the map, the right of way is irrefutable.

Right of way means that anyone may walk freely on a defined footpath or ride a horse or pedal cycle along a public bridleway.

South Downs Way sign

No one may interfere with this right and the walker is within his rights if he removes any obstruction along the route, provided that he has not set out purposely with the intention of removing that obstruction. All obstructions should be reported to the local Highways Authority.

In England and Wales rights of way fall into three main categories:

- Public Footpaths – for walkers only;

- Bridleways – for passage on foot, horseback, or bicycle;

- Byways – for all the above and for motorized vehicles

Free access to footpaths and bridleways does mean that certain guidelines should be followed as a courtesy to those who live and work in the area. For example, you should only sit down to picnic where it does not interfere with other walkers or the landowner. All gates must be kept closed to prevent stock from straying and dogs must be kept under close control – usually this is interpreted as meaning that they should be kept on a leash. Motor vehicles must not be driven along a public footpath or bridleway without the landowner's consent.

A farmer can put a docile mature beef bull with a herd of cows or heifers, in a field crossed by a public footpath. Beef bulls such as Herefords (usually brown/red colour) are unlikely to be upset by passers by but dairy bulls, like the black and white Friesian, can be dangerous by nature. It is, therefore, illegal for a farmer to let a dairy bull roam loose in a field open to public access.

The Countryside and Rights of Way Act 2000 (the 'right to roam') allows access on foot to areas of legally defined 'open country' – mountain, moor, downland, heath and registered common land. You will find these areas shaded orange on the maps in this guide. It does not allow freedom to walk anywhere. It also increases protection for Sites of Special Scientific Interest, improves wildlife enforcement legislation and allows better management of Areas of Outstanding Natural Beauty.

Amberley Wild Brooks

The Country Code

The Country Code has been designed not as a set of hard and fast rules, although they do have the backing of the law, but as a statement of commonsense. The code is a gentle reminder of how to behave in the countryside. Walkers should walk with the intention of leaving the place exactly as it was before they arrived. There is a saying that a good walker 'leaves only footprints and takes only photographs', which really sums up the code perfectly.

Never walk more than two abreast on a footpath as you will erode more ground by causing an unnatural widening of paths. Also try to avoid the spread of trodden ground around a boggy area. Mud soon cleans off boots but plant life is slow to grow back once it has been worn away.

Have respect for everything in the countryside, be it those beautiful flowers found along the way or a farmer's gate which is difficult to close.

Stone walls were built at a time when labour costs were a fraction of those today and the special skills required to build or repair them have almost disappeared. Never climb over or onto stone walls; always use stiles and gates.

Dogs which chase sheep can cause them to lose their lambs and a farmer is within his rights if he shoots a dog which he believes is worrying his stock.

The moors and woodlands are often tinder dry in summer, so take care not to start a fire. A fire caused by something as simple as a discarded cigarette can burn for weeks, once it gets deep down into the underlying peat.

When walking across fields or enclosed land, make sure that you read the map carefully and avoid trespassing. As a rule, the line of a footpath or right of way, even when it is not clearly defined on the ground, can usually be followed by lining up stiles or gates.

Obviously flowers and plants encountered on a walk should not be taken but left for others passing to enjoy. To use the excuse 'I have only taken a few' is futile. If everyone only took a few the countryside would be devastated. If young wild animals are encountered they should be left well alone. For instance, if a fawn or a deer calf is discovered lying still in the grass it would be wrong to assume that it has been abandoned. Mothers hide their offspring while they go away to graze and browse and return to them at feeding time. If the animals are touched it could mean that they will be abandoned as the human scent might deter the mother from returning to her offspring. Similarly with baby birds, who have not yet mastered flight; they may appear to have been abandoned but often are being watched by their parents who might be waiting for a walker to pass on before coming out to give flight lesson two!

What appear to be harmful snakes should not be killed because firstly the 'snake' could be a slow worm, which looks like a snake but is really a harmless legless lizard, and second, even if it were an adder (they are quite common) it will escape if given the opportunity. Adders are part of the pattern of nature and should not be persecuted. They rarely bite unless they are handled; a foolish act, which is not uncommon; or trodden on, which is rare, as the snakes are usually basking in full view and are very quick to escape.

Map reading

Some people find map reading so easy that they can open a map and immediately relate it to the area of countryside in which they are standing. To others, a map is as unintelligible as ancient Greek! A map is an accurate but flat picture of the three-dimensional features of the countryside. Features such as roads, streams, woodland and buildings are relatively easy to identify, either from their shape or position. Heights, on the other hand, can be difficult to interpret from the single dimension of a map. The Ordnance Survey 1:25,000 mapping used in this guide shows the contours at 5 metre intervals. Summits and spot heights are also shown.

The best way to estimate the angle of a slope, as shown on any map, is to remember that if the contour lines come close together then the slope is steep – the closer together the contours the steeper the slope.

Learn the symbols for features shown on the map and, when starting out on a walk, line up the map with one or more features, which are recognisable both from the map and on the ground. In this way, the map will be correctly positioned relative to the terrain. It should then only be necessary to look from the map towards the footpath or objective of your walk and then make for it! This process is also useful for determining your position at any time during the walk.

Let's take the skill of map reading one stage further: sometimes there are no easily recognisable features nearby: there may be the odd clump of trees and a building or two but none of them can be related exactly to the map. This is a frequent occurrence but there is a simple answer to the problem and this is where the use of a compass comes in. Simply place the map on the ground, or other flat surface, with the compass held gently above the map. Turn the map until the edge is parallel to the line of the compass needle, which should point to the top of the map. Lay the compass on the map and adjust the position of both, making sure that the compass needle still points to the top of the map and is parallel to the edge. By this method, the map is orientated in a north-south alignment. To find your position on the map, look out for prominent features and draw imaginary lines from them down on to the map. Your position is where these lines cross. This method of map reading takes a little practice before you can become proficient but it is worth the effort.

How to use this book

This book contains route maps and descriptions for 20 walks, with areas of interest indicated by symbols (see below). For each walk particular points of interest are denoted by a number both in the text and on the map (where the number appears in a circle). In the text the route instructions are prefixed by a capital letter. We recommend that you read the whole description, including the fact box at the start of each walk, before setting out.

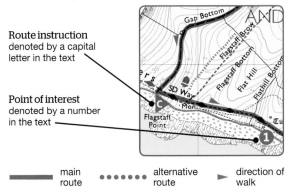

Route instruction denoted by a capital letter in the text

Point of interest denoted by a number in the text

—— main route

•••••••• alternative route

► direction of walk

Key to walk symbols

At the start of each walk there is a series of symbols that indicate particular areas of interest associated with the route.

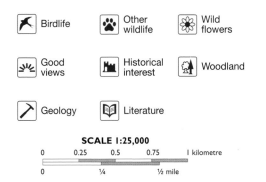

- Birdlife
- Other wildlife
- Wild flowers
- Good views
- Historical interest
- Woodland
- Geology
- Literature

SCALE 1:25,000

0   0.25   0.5   0.75   I kilometre

0   ¼   ½ mile

Please note the scale for walk maps is 1:25,000 unless otherwise stated
North is always at the top of the page

> **❝** An easy stroll through contrasting countryside starting and finishing at the delightful village green at Cheriton **❞**

The walk begins at Cheriton which lies on the B3046 between New Alresford on the A31 and New Cheriton on the A272. Park by the village green. This is a gentle walk on the very edge of the downland, an area brought to an end by the River Itchen, which runs down from the hills to the south of the village, turns sharply west, and then swings south again through Winchester to the sea. It is largely a peaceful, agricultural landscape of fields and meadows, though it has seen its moments of drama, for there was a Civil War battle fought in the area between Cheriton village and Cheriton Wood in 1644. Part of the walk follows the Cheriton Battlefield Walk.

Cheriton

Horse and Rider statue

Watford
LONDON
Reading
Basingstoke
Farnham
East Grinstead
Petersfield
Horsham
Brighton
Portsmouth
Eastbourne
Isle of Wight

DISTANCE: 3 miles (4.75km)

TIME: 2 hours

START/END: SU583284 Cheriton

TERRAIN: Easy

MAPS:
OS Explorer 132;
OS Landranger 185

Route instructions

A From the war memorial, walk along the road by the village green keeping the green on the right-hand side.

1 Cheriton village is a model of what an English village should be, the kind of place that exiles dream about in reveries of rural England. There are no striking individual features, but a happy combination of elements. Houses in a plain vernacular, using local materials, sit comfortably round the village green. The Itchen, here little more than a stream, runs through the green while ducks waddle over the grass or float on the clear water. There are memories of great antiquity, for the village church stands on a prehistoric mound. It all adds up to the sort of picture that has many times earned Cheriton the title of Best Kept Village in Hampshire.

B Turn left down Hill Houses Lane beside the high brick wall.

C Go through a wooden gate between two large metal gates and follow the path with the hedge on your right. Up the hill to your left is a sculpture of a horse and rider.

D Where the main path bears left uphill, carry straight on through a metal gate and walk down past Cheriton Mill to the road. Turn right over three white-railed bridges to the road.

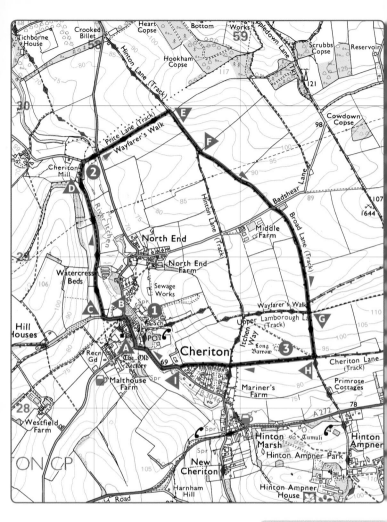

Cross straight across with the hedge to your right.

2 The walk out from Cheriton follows the line of the Itchen through rich, lush watermeadows. The river itself is lined with trees, through which the water is glimpsed as an occasional sparkle, while the meadows themselves are a delight, with long grasses dotted with flowers. This section ends at Cheriton Mill. It is a simple, but attractive red-brick building with a tiled roof, with an equally attractive mill house alongside.

Cheriton

E At the track junction, turn right.

F Where the track divides, take the left-hand fork. Carry on to cross the road by the large barn.

G Carry straight on through the height barrier. The Wayfarers Way leads off to the right here.

H At the second height barrier, turn right where the power lines cross overhead.

3 At this point on the walk, one could say that three quite distinct landscapes meet. The way itself passes through a sunken lane, part of a complex pattern of paths and tracks which have been in use since medieval times and probably earlier. This path links Cheriton to Cheriton Wood, which itself overlies an ancient field system. All around, you can see the gentle swellings of old grazing land, and this same path would have been used by shepherds to bring their flocks down to the Itchen valley.

In the field immediately to the north of the track is the prominent hump of a Neolithic long barrow or burial mound. Immediately south, however, there is a very different view. This is the formal parkland of Hinton Ampner House. The view is very much that of the 18th century, but the trees chosen for their contrasting beauties – lime, chestnut, maple and Turkey oak have mainly been planted in this century. So different generations have added their own distinctive features to this lovely landscape.

I Turn right at the road to return to Cheriton.

Agricultural landscape above Cheriton

> 66 The rolling landscape of the western extent of the South Downs contrasts sharply with the spectacular cliffs of Beachy Head and Seven Sisters further east 99

The walk begins at the village of West Meon, which is on the A32 1½ miles (2.5km) south of the junction with the A272. It covers an area of gently undulating agricultural land, dotted by woods and copses which, in its very gentleness, indicates that the Downs are coming to an end. If you think of the main range of the Downs as a long arm stretching west from Beachy Head, then here we have arrived at the hand, spreading out its fingers in different directions.

South Downs countryside

West Meon

Parish Church of
St John The Evangelist

Route instructions

1 West Meon village, like neighbouring East Meon, has been forced to squeeze itself into the narrow confines of the river valley. Here, however, there is even less free room for building, so the buildings that cannot find space in the valley have to straggle up and down the enclosing hillsides. They are, as one comes to expect in this part of the country, a charming collection of cottages and small houses, some thatched, some roofed with rich, red tiles.

The most prominent building is the village church, something of a newcomer to the scene for it was built in the 1840s. It is a splendid example of the Gothic Revival at its most exuberant, and is the work of one of the founders of the movement, George Gilbert Scott, the elder. The churchyard contains the graves of some famous people, including that of Thomas Lord. He provided the ground on which the newly formed Marylebone Cricket Club first played its matches two centuries ago – it was to become the headquarters of cricket, and still bears his name, Lord's. Here also is the grave of the parents of the famous political writer, William Cobbett, who described this same country in his famous book, Rural Rides.

A Start by turning up the minor road that runs

Plan your walk

Watford
LONDON
Reading
Basingstoke
East Grinstead
Farnham
Petersfield Horsham
Brighton
Portsmouth Eastbourne
Isle of Wight

DISTANCE: 4 miles (6.5km)

TIME: 2½ hours

START/END: SU640242 West Meon

TERRAIN: Moderate

MAPS:
OS Explorer 132;
OS Landranger 185

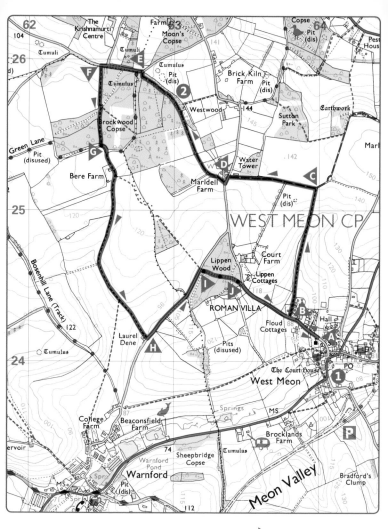

between the war memorial and the Red Lion.

B At the end of the houses, just before the end of a 30mph zone, turn right up the footpath indicated by a wooden sign.

C At the 'T' junction turn left.

D Turn left at the road and then immediately right on to the signposted bridleway.

2 Woodland and trees provide the dominant theme

West Meon

of this walk. After the long climb up from West Meon, with its wide vistas over the countryside, a magnificent avenue of beech trees leads you on to the woodland proper. Inevitably, parts of the woodland have been made over to conifers, but much of it remains as the older style of deciduous wood, with fine examples of that most typical of downland trees, the beech, mature oaks, and the real glory of the area, some splendid copper beeches.

E Turn left at the road.

F Pass a road on your right and then turn left. Follow the track along the side of the wood. Ignore the footpath marker on your left, walking straight on into the wood.

G At a 'T' junction in the path turn left, then bear right along the edge of the wood to a gate at Bere Farm. Walk past the house and through a gate on to a surfaced road.

H Turn left at the road.

I Walk along the road and walk for about 250yds (230m) after the start of the wood, turn right on to the wide, stony path through the wood. Cross over a surfaced road.

J At the next road, turn right to return to West Meon.

Brockwood Copse

> **The route uses contrasting paths – conventional tracks across fields, a deep, tree-shaded lane and the track bed of an old railway**

This walk begins at Corhampton on the A32. Turn west off the main road on to the B3035, Bishop's Waltham road, and then immediately right up a rough driveway to the church car park. This is a walk which offers tremendous variety of scenery, an equally varied type of footpath, and includes sites of historic interest that range through time from the Iron Age to the 19th century. The route moves out from the valley of the Meon to the top of a hill over 600ft (180m) above sea level, passing through both woodland and pasture.

Part of the walk follows the Monarch's Way – a long distance footpath following the escape route of Charles II to Shoreham after the Battle of Worcester in 1651.

View from Old Winchester Hill

Corhampton & Old Winchester Hill

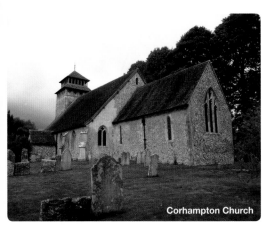

Corhampton Church

Route instructions

A From the car park, turn left on to the road then left again on to the main road.

B Turn right at the post office.

C Turn left at the 'T' junction, then right at the next 'T' junction.

D Turn right under the bridge and then left at the footpath sign up to the disused railway.

1 The railway line which now provides the footpath for the next ½ mile (800m) was once a branch line of the old London and South Western Railway, and originally ran from Basingstoke to Fareham, serving a dozen villages

along the way. Like many other routes, it fell victim to the 'Beeching Axe' which closed substantial numbers of branch lines in the 1950s.

Many of those are now finding a new use as walkways and cycle tracks and as a habitat for wild flowers, untroubled by the sprays and croppings of agricultural land. This section is part of a longer route that runs from Wickham for 9 miles (14.5km) to West Meon.

E At the bridge, go down steps on the right on to the path by the sunken lane. After a few yards, leave the South Downs way and go down on to the stony sunken lane.

Plan your walk

Watford
LONDON
Reading
Basingstoke
East
Farnham
Grinstead
Petersfield
Horsham
Brighton
Portsmouth
Eastbourne
Isle of Wight

DISTANCE: 5 miles (8 km)

TIME: 3 hours

START/END: SU610203 Corhampton

TERRAIN: Moderately difficult; quite strenuous between points F and G

MAPS:
OS Explorer 119;
OS Landranger 185

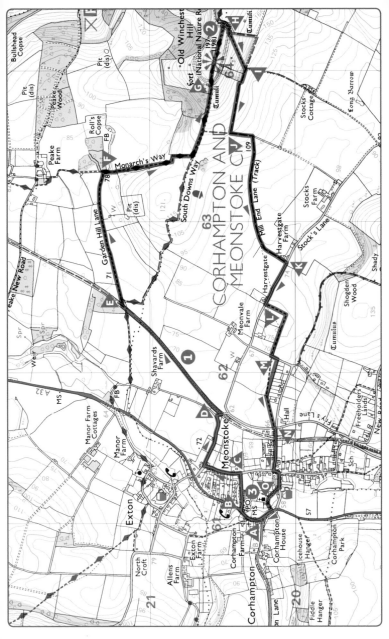

Corhampton & Old Winchester Hill

F At the concrete track at the edge of the wood, turn right. At the fork in the track go left and follow the right edge of the field. At the top, turn left and walk between the fence and the trees.

G Walk through the earthworks to the obvious gap at the other side of the plateau.

2 Old Winchester Hill is crowned by the last of the great Iron Age hill forts that dot the tops of the downland hills.

The fort itself has an area of some 14 acres (5.5 ha), enclosed by rampart and ditch. The earthworks have ramparts rising to 15ft (4.5m) above the ditch, and with two clearly defined entrances at the eastern and western ends. The whole site is now a nature reserve.

H Turn right and follow the edge of the earthworks on a green path. Go through a gate on the left to follow the track downhill diagonally to the right.

I At the foot of the hill, go through the kissing gate and take the path to the right marked 'South Downs Way'.

J At the South Downs Way signpost turn left keeping the hedge on your left. Then turn right at the Bridleway sign around the edge of the field.

K Turn right at the road.

L Turn left into the field at the footpath sign opposite the brick house. Cross the stile through the trees down to the road.

M Cross the stile opposite, and head for the stile in the left-hand corner of the field. Continue across the next field to the gate by the road.

N At the crossroads, take the road straight ahead over the hump-backed railway bridge. Follow the road left then right.

O Take the road on the right before the Bucks Head, past the church to the main road. Turn right and return to the car park.

3 Corhampton's Saxon church has no dedication to any saint; it is simply Corhampton Church. The most striking features are the wall paintings, which are most likely to be 12th century.

There are interesting features outside. The sundial by the south porch is marked out to record the Saxon day, divided into eight instead of our familiar twelve units. The churchyard also boasts an ancient, massive yew tree.

> *"A walk through the typical English countryside of shady country lanes, woodland and pasture"*

Buriton is an attractive village reached by a minor road that turns east off the A3, slightly more than a mile (1.6km) south of Petersfield. There is adequate parking in the village, particularly in the area where the walk starts by the village pond and the church. This route comes right up to the edge of the county boundary between Hampshire and West Sussex and does not boast the drama of wide vistas that are such a mark of the routes that touch the top of the chalk ridge, but instead offers the quieter pleasures of shady country lanes, woodland, and pasture.

Tree-lined country lane leading to Buriton

Buriton Village & Coulters Dean Nature Reserve

St Mary's Church, Buriton

Route instructions

1 The village of Buriton is quite large, but is still dominated by the twin pillars of village life, church and manor house. The latter is a fine establishment, looking out over pasture, where grazing sheep dot the green. It is chiefly remembered today as the former home of the famous historian, Edward Gibbon. The church is unusually grand for a village, but once served a wide area, including the parish of Petersfield. It is handsome, if unpretentious, and has a set of Ringers' Rules in the bell tower which begins:

Advice to ringers and to such:
That delight in bells and love ye Church;

Beware of oaths and quarrelings;
Take heed of clams and janglings;
There is no musik played or sung;
Like unto bells if they are well rung.

The scene created by manor, church, and shady village pond is one of the most delightful to be met on the whole South Downs.

A Take the road past the war memorial, North Lane.

B Bear right onto Pitcroft Lane and walk past the large black Buriton Estate gates.

C Stay on the path and bear left beneath the

Plan your walk

DISTANCE: 4 miles (6.5km)

TIME: 2½ hours

START/END: SU740201 Buriton

TERRAIN: Moderate; muddy when wet

MAPS:
OS Explorer 133;
OS Landranger 197

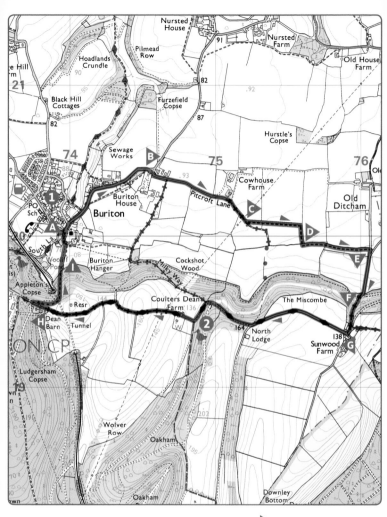

electricity lines. Walk around the edge of the field to a bridge in the corner.

D Cross the bridge and turn left along the edge of the field past a small barn to the road.

E Turn right onto the road.

F Where the road bends to the left at the edge of the wood, bear right following the byway sign and continue straight up the hill to meet the South Downs Way at the road.

G Turn right and stay on the South Downs Way all

Buriton Village & Coulters Dean Nature Reserve

the way past Coulters Dean Nature Reserve and carry on beneath the electricity lines.

2 Coulters Dean Nature Reserve covers 11 acres (4ha) and comprises woodland and chalk grassland which would, at one time, have covered much of Hampshire. The round-headed rampion can be found thriving on chalky grassland. It is now quite rare not only because of the increase in farming but also the encroachment of scrubland on the hillsides due to the reduced levels of grazing. There are also many species of butterfly including common spotted and fragrant orchid. The oddly named cheese snail can be found in

the woodland. Cowslips are in abundance in the spring and orchids such as butterfly, common spotted and fragrant orchid can be seen during the summer. The reserve is open all year.

H Pass several houses and stay on the South Downs Way uphill. At a footpath sign almost at the brow of the hill, turn right into the woods. Immediately, the path forks. Take the right fork downhill, passing the railway tunnel entrance on your left.

I Emerge from the trees and head across the field to a gate in the gap in the trees. Cross onto the road and turn left back to the village pond and church.

Buriton village pond

The walk begins at the village of Rowlands Castle, which lies to the east of the B2149, Horndean to Havant road. There is ample parking space either in the village streets, in the station car park or on the east side of the railway viaduct. Rowlands Castle owes its name to a Norman motte and bailey castle, the remains of which can be seen to the south of the town. The forest itself was once the hunting ground of medieval kings, where Henry II had a hunting lodge built. Today, this is mixed woodland in which the different uses are indicated by the old names of the different sections: Firtree Piece, Oak Copse and Hare Warren.

Stansted Forest & Park

The Avenue

Route instructions

A Walk through the main arch of the railway viaduct and take the left fork past the Castle Inn.

B Where the road turns left, take the footpath on the right. Carry straight on past the large tree at the four-way crossing on to the avenue of trees and continue towards Stansted House.

1 The broad tree-lined avenue, known as 'The Avenue', leads from Rowlands Castle all the way up to Stansted House. Visitors to the great house in the 18th century could see all the way down from the dining room to the tall masts of the ships in Portsmouth Harbour.

The Avenue itself was once a good deal more impressive than it is today, for it was bordered by giant beech trees which sadly succumbed to disease in the 1970s. At the point where The Avenue crosses the road, the entrance to Stansted Park is marked by an ornate gatehouse. From here, it is possible to believe that one was looking along to an elegant Georgian manor but, in fact, the original was burned down in 1900 and then reconstructed. After this grand parade down towards Stansted House, the walk turns off into the woods, and remains a pleasant saunter through the trees all the way round and back to Rowlands Castle.

Plan your walk

DISTANCE: 3½ miles (5.5km)

TIME: 2 hours

START/END: SU735108 Rowlands Castle

TERRAIN: Easy; muddy when wet

MAPS: OS Explorer 120; OS Landranger 197

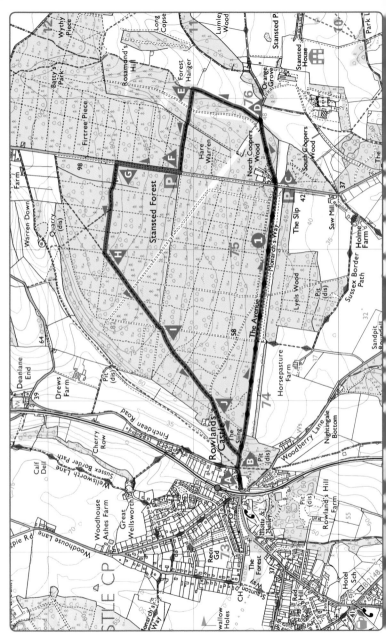

Stansted Forest & Park

C Cross the road. Go through the gates next to Middle Lodge and take the path into Stansted Park.

D At the edge of the wood, turn left through the gate on to the bridleway, just before the speed bump marked by posts.

E Just after the path becomes lined with trees on both sides, turn left across a stile at a waymark into the woods. Cross two tracks to the road.

F Turn right at the road.

G At the public footpath signpost, turn left across the stile on to the track.

H Keep walking past several crossing paths until you arrive at a six-way crossing point. Take the second path on the left. There is a waymark in the ferns in the middle.

I Where a second broad green track crosses the path, turn left and then immediately right following the footpath sign.

J Turn right on to the surfaced road and return to the start.

Middle Lodge gatehouse

66 Kingley Vale is famed for its dense woodland summed up by Wordsworth as 6Like leafless underboughs in some thick wood, All withered by the depth of shade above9. (from *The Excursion*) 99

Kingley Vale is reached by taking a turning to the north off the B2178 at East Ashling, where the road makes a right-angled turn. At the T-junction, turn left and the car park is immediately on the right.

Kingley Vale Nature Reserve

Bronze Age burial mounds

Plan your walk

DISTANCE: 3¾ miles (6 km)

TIME: 2 hours

START/END: SU824088 Signposted car park just west of West Stoke

TERRAIN: Moderately strenuous at times and very muddy in wet weather

MAPS: OS Explorer 120; OS Landranger 197

Route instructions

A The footpath starts at the stile in the corner of the car park.

B At the edge of the nature reserve at the striking sculpture, the 'Spirit of Kingley Vale', go through the kissing gate and follow the green path round to the left. Keep on this path around the edge of the wood.

1 The principal feature of the Kingley Vale Nature Reserve is the yew tree grove, which is said to be the finest of its kind in Europe. Some of the trees are as much as 500 years old. Much of the forest is quite dense, and the path follows the rim of the vale where the trees cling to the precipitous hillside. They give

an idea of what it may have been like when woodland covered most of Britain.

C At the nature trail '24' signpost (it has its back to you), take the track bearing round to the right.

2 At the top of the hill is the superb row of Bronze Age burial mounds, or barrows, known as the Devil's Humps. The views from here are also very fine, looking out over the Downs to the north to Butser Hill and south to Chichester and the Isle of Wight.

D Stay on the track past the tumuli and Bow Hill on your left. At the four-way fingerpost turn sharp right downhill.

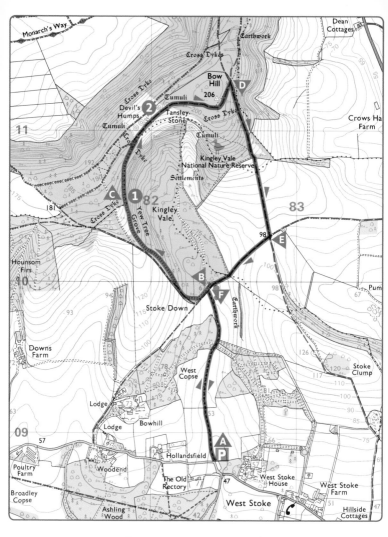

E Walk into open countryside and carry on downhill. Where the paths cross, turn right.

F Walk back to the stile leading to the nature reserve and the 'Spirit of Kingley Vale'. Turn left and return to the car park.

Kingley Vale
Nature Reserve

Kingley Vale Nature Reserve

66 Two pleasant villages and a climb to get the heart pumping are the rewards on this walk of mixed scenery and gradient **99**

The walk begins at Cocking village on the A286. It is possible to park in the village on the roads leading off the main road near the post office, but please ensure you park considerately. The two villages of Cocking and Heyshott, encountered on the walk, have very different characters, as do the different sections of the walk itself.

The first part is a gentle stroll through farmland at the foot of the Downs. This is followed by a steep climb up through woodlands to join the South Downs Way, which is then followed along the crest of the hill, until another steep path takes you down again and back to the start.

Parish church of

Cocking & Heyshott Down

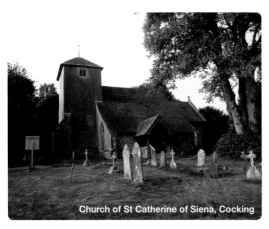
Church of St Catherine of Siena, Cocking

Route instructions

A The walk starts at the post office in Cocking. Take the minor road that runs off the A286 alongside the post office.

B After a few yards, continue straight on at the public footpath sign.

C Cross the bridge and bear left with the stream on your left. Turn right with the fence on your left and walk alongside the garage. At the end of the fence turn right at the fingerpost. Climb steps and walk around the edge of the field.

D At Sages Barn go to the left around the house to the waymarked post. Carry on across the field.

E At the road turn right and, just before the road junction, go up steps on the left into the field. Follow the waymarks to the wood.

F Pass through the wood (Hampshire Copse) and follow the waymarks across several fields.

G Finally, climb a stile on to a surfaced road and turn left past Leggs Farm towards Heyshott.

1 Heyshott is one of those villages which seem scarcely touched by the modern world. It is tucked away in a sheltered hollow, hemmed in by the woodland of the Weald and the steeply rising slopes of the Downs. Once it had its moated manor, but

Plan your walk

DISTANCE: 3¾ miles (6km)

TIME: 2½ hours

START/END: SU878177 Cocking

TERRAIN: Strenuous

MAPS:
OS Explorer 120;
OS Landranger 197

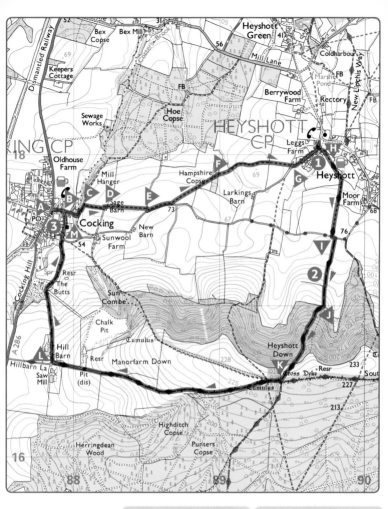

now it is a cluster of farms, cottages, a village green, and a memorial inside records its most famous parishioner, Richard Cobden, leader of the Anti Corn Law League.

It seems odd to think that the man who fought so hard against the agricultural interest of Victorian England should himself have lived in such a remote, rural village. The church can also boast three fine, antique bells, the oldest having been cast at the end of the 14th century.

H At the last building on the right before the church (Cobden Club Hall), turn right

Cocking & Heyshott Down

and follow the path across the field, following the Lipchis Way signs. Where the hedge turns left, carry straight on across the field to steps leading up to a lane.

▶ Turn left and after 30yds (27m), turn right to take the green lane straight up the hillside.

2 The approach to Heyshott Down is along a sunken lane, the high banks topped by hedges, rich with hedgerow plants and with a rich variety of butterflies to be seen in early summer. Mixed woodland, predominantly beech and oak, covers the hillside and the air is sweetened by clumps of wild rose and honeysuckle. At the top of the Downs, the open hillside is also made colourful by patches of heather, a plant rarely found on the chalk. It was this, in fact, which gave Heyshott its name, which literally means 'Corner in the Heather'. Charlton Forest which blankets the countryside to the south is home to deer, which can often be seen grazing at the edge of the trees, though they scamper off for cover very rapidly when humans appear.

▶ Just before the information board, turn right and follow the path uphill to the top of the ridge.

▶ At the edge of the woods, bear right to the corner of the field and the broad track of the South Downs Way. Turn right and follow the Way for 1 mile (1.6km).

▶ Beyond the pair of cottages, turn right past a group of barns and on to a rutted track. Continue downhill past 'The Butts'.

▶ Join the road and go through the churchyard. Turn left to follow the road back to the post office.

3 The descent into Cocking goes steeply downhill past a still-worked chalkpit to emerge by the clear, bubbling water of a spring. Beside it stands the village church, which is really quite grand. It is well worth exploring, if only to see the 13th century wall painting of the angel appearing to the shepherds at the Nativity. The anonymous painter clearly took the men of the downs as his model; they are shown with their sheepdog, and one of the shepherds carries an old-style Sussex crook. It was dedicated to St Catherine of Siena in 2007. For the previous 900 years it had been called simply Cocking Church with no dedication to any saint.

> 66 A gentle walk around a complex of
> two man-made 16th century lakes,
> heathland and woodland 99

Burton Pond is a nature reserve managed jointly by West Sussex County Council and the Sussex Trust for Nature Conservation. The walk takes place mainly within the confines of the reserve, and incorporates the mill pond itself, the common and woodland on either side. It also includes a brief look at the River Rother. To reach the start take the A285 south from Petworth and, after 2 miles (3.25km) take a turn to the left, sign posted Burton Mill. The nature reserve car park is a mile (1.5km) along the road, just after a sharp left hand bend on the left just before you cross the pond itself. Note that there are no facilities at the reserve.

Burton Mill Pond & The Rother Valley

Chingford Pond

Route instructions

1 Burton Mill had long been disused, but was restored and put back to work in 1978, It has also been open to the public as a museum but it is now in private ownership and not open to the public. It has an interesting history. The first and most obvious feature is the enormous mill pond which was originally constructed to provide water for a wheel that would work the massive hammers of an iron forge. The grain mill was built in 1781 with two water wheels, but these were replaced by water turbines earlier this century.

A From the car park, turn right at the road and go through the white gates for Barton Mill Lodge. Go up to the road and take the footpath beside the pond through the white gate.

B At the road turn left.

C Carry straight on along the signed footpath.

D After crossing Chingford pond, bear right at a waymarked post.

2 The path passes through parkland, which was landscaped in the 18th century, and the sweet chestnuts which were planted at that time have now grown to massive proportions. Another landscape feature is the ornamental lake, Chingford Pond. The path crosses a

Plan your walk

Watford
LONDON
Reading
Basingstoke
East Grinstead
Farnham
Petersfield Horsham
Brighton
Portsmouth Eastbourne
Isle of Wight

DISTANCE: 3 miles (4.75km)

TIME: 2 hours

START/END: SU979180 Burton Mill Nature Reserve car park

TERRAIN: Easy

MAPS:
OS Explorer 121;
OS Landranger 197

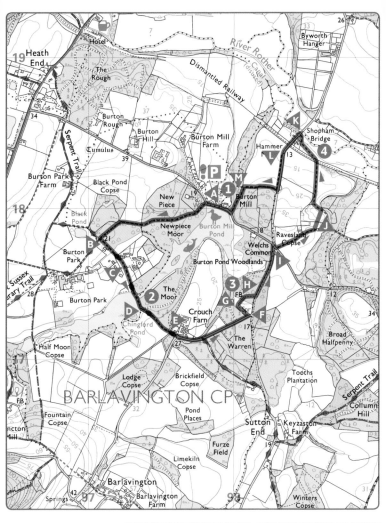

causeway between this and the hammer pond, and it is interesting to compare the two. The ornamental lake has suitably picturesque, uneven boundaries, and there are the remains of a grotto and cascade by the path, while the latter is strictly functional. Both are home to a variety of waterbirds, which have made their home among the reeds, including grebe, mallard, coot, and moorhen

E At the end of the wood, cross the track, keep

Burton Mill Pond & The Rother Valley

straight on past the farmhouse and turn left on to the road.

F 30yds (27m) before the road junction, turn left on to a narrow path through the wood.

G Turn right on to the boards across the bog – 'The Black Hole'.

3 A causeway takes walkers safely through the peat bog in the middle of the woodland of Welch's Common. There are a number of rare water plants to be seen here, such as the delicate pink and white bogbean. The woodland of birch, oak, and alder is home to fallow and roe deer, but these shy creatures are rarely seen. Far more common and very visible are the wood ants that swarm over the pathways in the drier parts of the woodland.

H Turn right at the end of the boards back up to the road. Turn left.

I At the crossroads, take the footpath just to the right and follow in the direction indicated by the sign.

J Cross the stile and walk to the left of the telegraph pole. Head uphill to a stile in the corner of the field. Keep to the left edge of the field.

4 The walk encounters two disused transport systems. The first is a cutting on what was a branch line of the London, Brighton, and South Coast Railway from Midhurst to Pulborough. The tracks have gone but the banks of the cutting make an ideal home for rabbits which can be seen scampering all over the old line. The River Rother was made navigable by artificial cuttings in the 1790s. It has long since become disused, and the canalized sections have dried up, leaving only the peaceful natural river.

K Turn left at the bridge.

L Just beyond the railway bridge, turn right into the field and follow the path round the edge. Cross the stile in the corner and turn right between the trees and the fence.

M Turn left into the wood and return to the road. Turn right back to the car park.

River Rother

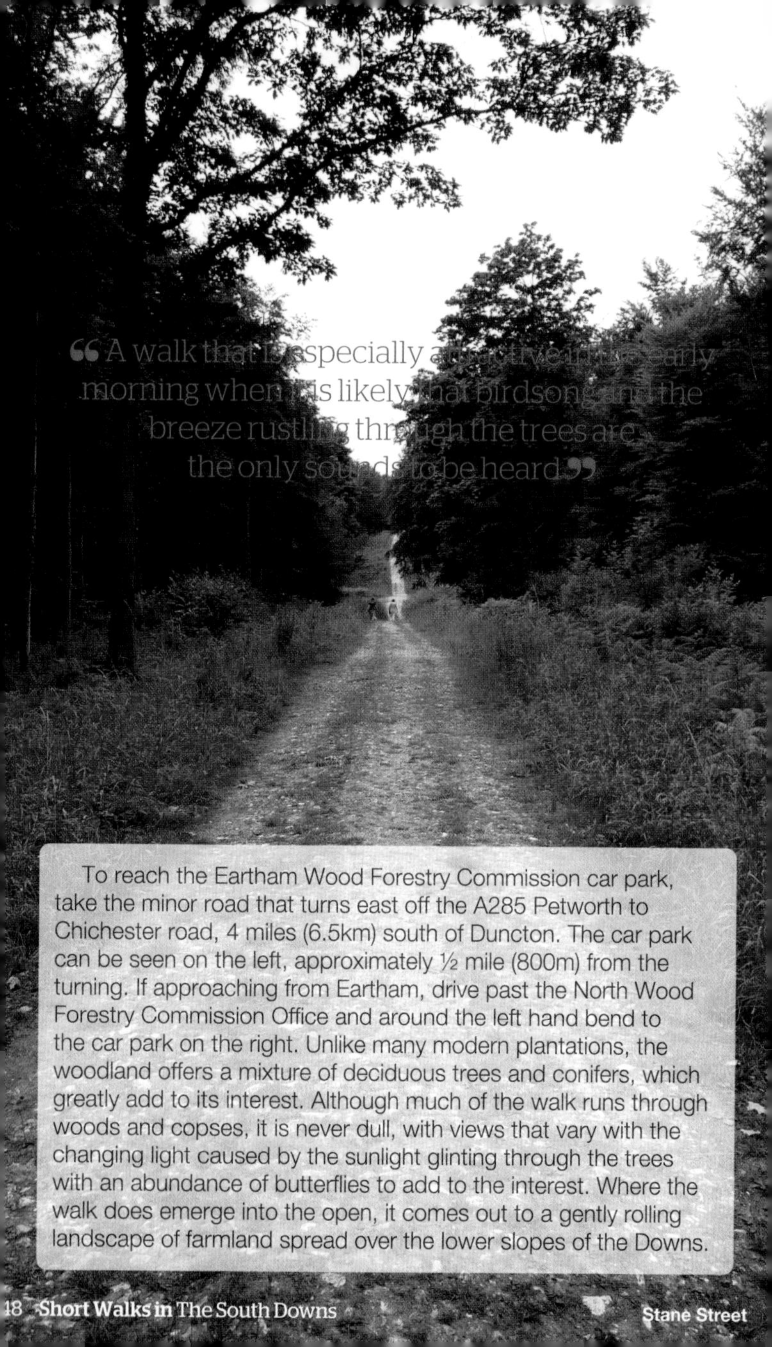

A walk that is especially attractive in the early morning when it is likely that birdsong and the breeze rustling through the trees are the only sounds to be heard

To reach the Eartham Wood Forestry Commission car park, take the minor road that turns east off the A285 Petworth to Chichester road, 4 miles (6.5km) south of Duncton. The car park can be seen on the left, approximately ½ mile (800m) from the turning. If approaching from Eartham, drive past the North Wood Forestry Commission Office and around the left hand bend to the car park on the right. Unlike many modern plantations, the woodland offers a mixture of deciduous trees and conifers, which greatly add to its interest. Although much of the walk runs through woods and copses, it is never dull, with views that vary with the changing light caused by the sunlight glinting through the trees with an abundance of butterflies to add to the interest. Where the walk does emerge into the open, it comes out to a gently rolling landscape of farmland spread over the lower slopes of the Downs.

Eartham Wood & Stane Street

Eartham Wood

Route instructions

A Starting in the car park facing the road, take the path to the left, through the wooden posts.

B At the broad gravel path, turn right for 30yds (27m) and then left at the public bridleway sign on to Stane Street.

1 Stane Street is a roman road, which ran from Londinium, or London, to Regnum, present-day Chichester. It heads straight uphill without a sign of any deviation, all the way to the horizon, and appears as a broad track raised on a slight embankment above the level of the surrounding country.

All this section of the road is well preserved and shows typical Roman engineering techniques. The surface was laid on top of an embankment, or agger which, in some sections on this walk, is as much as 50ft (15m) wide and 4ft (1.2m) high. This provided good drainage which was improved by ditches cut at the sides of the road, which can still be seen. It would originally have been surfaced with broken flint and gravel. But even this short section impresses one with the skill of the military engineers of nearly 2000 years ago. Six bridleways meet near the edge of Eartham Wood, and it can be clearly seen that our route has a different character from the rest.

Plan your walk

DISTANCE: 4½ miles (7.25 km)

TIME: 3 hours

START/END: SU938107 Eartham Wood Forestry Commission car park

TERRAIN: Moderate

MAPS:
OS Explorer 121;
OS Landranger 197

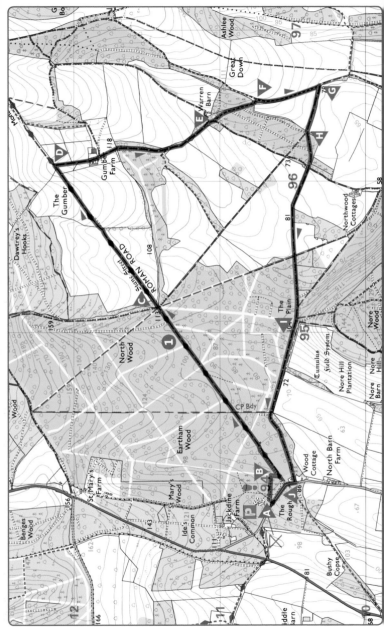

Eartham Wood & Stane Street

C After the six bridleways crossing point, follow the tree-lined path to emerge at several gates. Carry straight on through the wooden gate following the Monarch's Way sign.

D Turn right and head down past the barns of Gumber Farm.

E Where the path divides by a pond and an old walled garden, take the route to the left through the wood.

F At the edge of the wood, take the green path to the right, with the trees on your right and open fields to your left.

G Take the signed rutted track to the right 50yds (46m) beyond the stile.

H At the next patch of woodland, take the path to the left, following the blue waymarks.

I Walk across the clearing and carry straight on to re-enter the woodland.

J Walk through the Forestry Commission offices car park, turn right at the road and return to the car park.

Silver-washed fritillary

> **❝** Amberley Wild Brooks sits on the floodplain of the River Arun and is an area of largely unspoilt wet grassland, intersected by man-made ditches rich in wildlife **❞**

The walk begins in Amberley village, where there is on-street parking. This is quite unlike most of the other walks, and the name of the area covered – 'Amberley Wild Brooks' – gives a good idea of what to expect, even though it is, in fact, a corruption of 'Weald Brooks'. This is an area of watermeadows, swamp and peat bog, rich with a varied flora, ranging from the bold colours of the yellow flag to the delicate bog rosemary. In summer it is busy with insects and waterfowl, including large flocks of geese. This walk can be combined with a contrasting downland excursion at Rackham Banks, Walk 11.

Amberley Wild Brooks

Amberley

Plan your walk

Watford
LONDON
Reading
Basingstoke
Farnham
East Grinstead
Petersfield
Horsham
Brighton
Portsmouth
Eastbourne
Isle of Wight

DISTANCE: 5 miles (8km)

TIME: 3 hours

START/END: TQ031133 Amberley

TERRAIN: Easy; boggy in parts

MAPS:
OS Explorer 121;
OS Landranger 197

Route instructions

1 Amberley village is one of the most attractive to be found along the whole Downs. It is a perfect example of a traditional Sussex village, with a wealth of attractive thatched houses' and cottages. The approach is dominated by the castle which occupies a site that has been fortified since before the Norman Conquest. The main fortifications date from the 14th century, when a great hall was built and a moat constructed. Over the years, it has been added to so that it has gradually changed from a dour, defensive stronghold to the family home seen today.

The other focal point is St Michael's Church, a very grand affair for such a small place, but reflecting the fact that the castle was home to the bishops of Selsey. It is predominantly Norman, and contains some slightly faded medieval wall paintings telling the story of the crucifixion.

A Starting in Amberley, take the road with the Black Horse Inn on your right and the White House on your left and walk out of the village towards Rackham.

B Pass The Sportsman and, at the end of the houses, cross a stile. Take the well-defined footpath across the fields. Cross two wooden bridges and then a stile. Turn left through the wood.

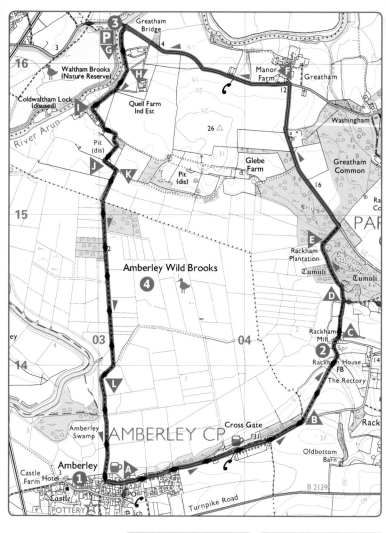

2 Rackham Mill stands at the boundary between the rising, dry ground on which Rackham stands and the watermeadows of the Wild Brooks. Grain from the surrounding farms was brought here to be ground into flour, the millstones being turned by an overshot waterwheel – the water from a trough or 'launder' falls on to the top of the wheel, the force and weight of the water driving the wheel round.

Amberley Wild Brooks

From here, the walk goes on into an area of woodland – partly traditional downland species dominated by beech and oak, and partly modern coniferous plantation.

C At Rackham Mill, cross the stile and head towards the woods following the line of the stream.

D Bear right into the woods and cross a footbridge. Turn left and follow the path keeping the fence to your left.

E The path veers away from the fields. Carry straight on to the road and turn left.

F Turn left at the road junction.

3 Greatham Bridge marked the old limit of navigation of the River Arun, and barges could still make their way this far up river right into the present century. The river here is tidal, with a rise of some 4ft (1.2m) at spring tides, hence the need for protective flood banks.

G Just before the bridge turn left across the stile and follow the river bank.

H Leave the river to the left of the woodland and go up on to a gravel track.

I At the edge of the woodland, turn left and stay on the path until you turn right at a small wood.

J Go through a wooden gate and immediately turn left at the public footpath sign.

K Go through the gate into the field, and turn right through Amberley Wild Brooks, keeping to the track between the two drainage ditches.

4 The final part of the walk is on a track across the bogs and marshes of the Wild Brooks. The straight lines of the drainage ditches show human attempts to tame and control this wasteland. It has been, at best, a partially successful attempt, and any straying from the track can lead to a walker disappearing over the ankles in thick, cloying ooze or peaty brown slime. The rewards come, however, in walking an area which can convey a real sense of loneliness, with an atmosphere much closer to that of the fens of East Anglia. Trees line the drainage ditches and cattle graze on reclaimed land, but elsewhere the only inhabitants seem to be the birds and insects.

L Keep heading south until you cross a stile next to a metal gate. Shortly after the path bears right, stay on the path to the road and return to the start.

> **A walk covering part of the South Downs Way itself and then exploring the rich, undulating country to the south of the ridge**

This particular walk is very much a downland route and can easily be combined with Walk 10, for a contrasting day featuring both downland and watermeadows. The final section of the route takes you down a beautiful, steep sided valley that is in stark contrast to the open scenery around Rackham Hill and Rackham Banks, the remains of ancient earthworks.

There are two possible start points for this walk – Amberley Station/Museum and Heritage Centre and in Amberley village. If you intend using the museum car park, we would ask that you contact the museum beforehand to obtain permission. Note that the car park is locked when the museum closes. It is also possible to park on High Titten (see map).

Valley beneath Rackham Hill

Rackham Banks

Rackham Hill

Route instructions

Watford

LONDON

Reading

Basingstoke

Farnham

East Grinstead

Petersfield

Horsham

Brighton

Portsmouth

Eastbourne

Isle of Wight

DISTANCE: 5 miles
(8km)

TIME: 3 hours

START/END: TQ027118
Amberley Museum and
Heritage Centre or
TQ031133 Amberley
Village

TERRAIN: Moderate

MAPS:
OS Explorer 121;
OS Landranger 197

1 The Amberley Museum
and Heritage Centre is
a 36 acre (14.5ha) site
which tells the story of
the industrial heritage of
the area. It is home to a
collection of buildings
that have been saved
and restored as well as
transport collections and
resident craftspeople such
as blacksmiths, potters,
woodturners, and a walking
stick maker amongst many
others. There are many
special events throughout
the year including vintage
car and motorcycle shows,
steam days and craft and
food festivals. It is run
largely by volunteers and
also includes a nature trail,
restaurant and gift shop.
The museum is open
Tuesday to Sunday from

February until the end of
October and on some
selected Mondays.

A Make your way to the
intersection of High Titten
and the Wey South Path
at **B**.

B At the road junction,
if walking up High Titten,
turn right; or if the start point
was in Amberley, carry
straight on. Head east uphill
on the South Downs Way.
Bear left to continue on
the South Downs Way to
Rackham Banks.

C At the earthworks on
the left with prominent bank
and ditch, turn right off the
South Downs way keeping
to the left of the woodland.
To your left is Rackham Hill.

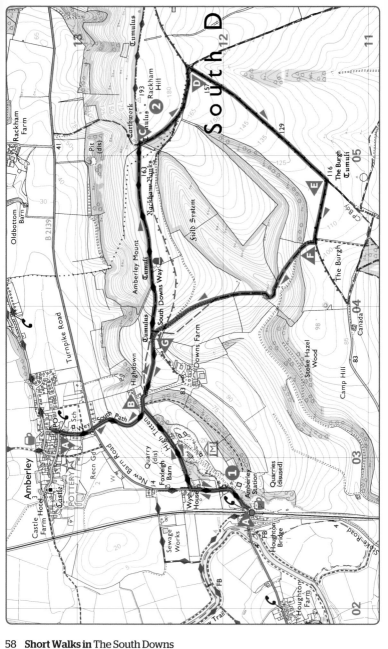

Rackham Banks

2 Rackham Hill, the high point of this walk, commands extensive views over the Arun valley. Here, the path is crossed by the Rackham Banks, impressive earthworks, the exact purpose of which is unknown. However, it is thought that they may have been boundary markers. In 1929 a fragment of pottery found at the site gave the indication that the works date from the late bronze age. It is unfortunate that much of the site has been substantially flattened by farming over the many years since but an indication of how impressive they must have been can still be gained.

D Carry straight on past the path coming in from your right. Carry on to a track. Turn right downhill through the metal gate.

E At the junction, turn right following the public right of way signpost.

F At a four-way crossing, take the path to the right. The contrast in scenery as you turn into the valley is quite startling. Follow the path down into the valley and up the other side. After emerging from the valley, where the path splits into two it is best to stay to the right path.

G At the South Downs Way, turn left and retrace your steps to your start point.

Valley below Rackham Hill

> **&6** Although never far from the busy A27, there is much variety and interest from the eccentricity of 'The Miller's Tale' to the ancient hillfort and the tranquility of Highdown Gardens **99**

To reach Highdown Hill, turn north off the A259, Worthing to Littlehampton road, a little way west of the roundabout to the north of Goring. The minor road is well signposted to Highdown Hotel and Highdown Gardens but it only accessible from the eastbound carriageway. Carry on as far as the road takes you, to the car park next to the gardens – which have free access. The walk offers a mixture of downland, woods, and fields but does involve two crossings of the busy A27 trunk road.

Highdown Hill & Clapham Village

Highdown Hill hill fort

Route instructions

1 Highdown Gardens are one of Sussex's undiscovered treasures. It is a beautiful 8.5 acre (3.4ha) garden with views out to sea. It was created from an old chalk pit and includes variety such as ponds, trees and shrubs, herb and rose gardens and beech woods amongst many others. It was created by Sir Frederick Stern in the early 20th century and was passed into the care of Worthing borough council on his death in 1967. Admission is free and is open all year round although not at weekends during the winter.

A Leave the car park through the gate next to Highdown Gardens entrance.

Walk past the Miller's Tomb and the unusual seat carved from a tree. Go through a kissing gate and head for the hill fort.

2 John Olliver was an eccentric, wealthy miller who lived a little way down the slope from here. He built this tomb 27 years before his death in 1793 at the age of 84. Towards the end of his life he spent many hours in a small hut that he built at the head of the tomb. His funeral was attended by over 2000 people and his white coffin was brought to his final resting place by eight white-robed ladies. It is said that running seven times around the tomb will summon his ghost.

Plan your walk

DISTANCE: 4½ miles (7.25km)

TIME: 2½ hours

START/END: TQ099041 Car park at Highdown Gardens

TERRAIN: Moderate; very muddy in wet weather

MAPS: OS Explorer 121; OS Landranger 198

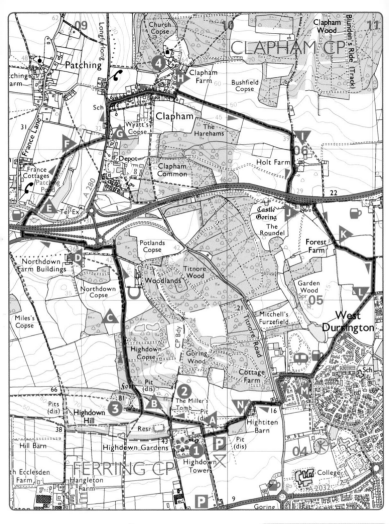

B From the hill fort, retrace your steps and turn left at a public bridleway sign, around the edge of the depression and into the woods.

3 Highdown Hill, like most isolated hills in Sussex, was fortified in the Iron Age. The ramparts and ditches are impressive, but they only enclose a small area. It is now a popular spot with visitors who enjoy the fine sea views, and, on a clear day, you can see as far as Beachy Head to the east and the Isle of Wight to the west.

Highdown Hill & Clapham Village

C Emerge at a broad track and carry straight on. Take the next footpath on the left, just before the road.

D Cross the A27 and turn left to the lay-by. Follow the path alongside the road. At the end turn right under the bridge.

E Cross the road and take the footpath to the right of the Worlds End pub. Cross a stile into an open field.

F Just after passing a stile on your left, bear right to the edge of the trees. At the stile, follow the path uphill to the marker post, and past the village hall.

G At the road, turn left and then right into Clapham village. A detour can be made to the church which is signposted off The Street.

4 The village of Clapham is centred on a single dead end road called The Street. The housing seems mostly quite modern giving the indication that this is a relatively new settlement, until you realise that Clapham originated around the church a little further to the north. The church of St Mary the Virgin sits on the edge of woodland and dates mainly from the 12th and 13th centuries, and contains 16th century memorial brasses to the ancestors of the poet Shelley.

H Walk through the village to a public footpath sign at the last house. Turn left then after 20yds (18m) right through a metal gate.

I Cross a stile onto a track and turn right past the farm buildings to the A27.

J Go straight across the A27 to the bus stop and through the trees onto a lane. Turn left and follow the track as it veers right away from the A27.

K At the houses, bear left along the edge of a field. Turn right at the signpost.

L At the footpath signpost, by the houses, bear right across the field to the right of Tesco and emerge at a mini-roundabout. Carry on into Fulbeck Avenue. Bear right at a public footpath sign and follow the path behind The Trout public house.

M Bear right down Titmore Way. Go through metal barriers on your left before the road. Walk along the path to wooden barriers on your right. Cross the road to the concrete track opposite.

N Stay to the right of the grey silos and the tithe barn and walk up the footpath through a wooden gate. Stay to the left and head back to the car park.

Turn south off the A283, Steyning to Storrington road, about 2½ miles (4km) west of Steyning on to a narrow, unclassified road signposted to Chanctonbury. The car park and picnic area are at the foot of the Downs. The climb up through the woods to join the South Downs Way is strenuous but rewarding and from there, it is largely gently downhill all the way back to the start. Good paths are followed all the way round.

Sunlit trees at Combe Holt

Chanctonbury Ring & Washington

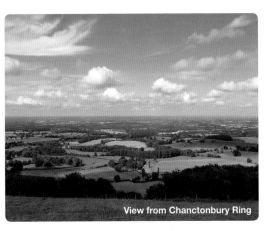

View from Chanctonbury Ring

Route instructions

A Turn left out of the picnic area and follow the path heading straight on towards the hill. Then climb up the hill on the public bridleway through the wood.

1 The walk up to the summit of the Downs is along a well-marked track (Wiston Bostal) through mixed woodland. Over to the left here are occasional glimpses of Wiston House, home of Charles Goring who planted the Chanctonbury beeches.

B At the top of the ridge, turn right on to the South Downs Way and walk past the Chanctonbury Ring.

2 At the top of the Downs, the walk joins the South Downs Way in an area of open grassland. There are fine views over the Weald to the north and southwards past the prominent, isolated Cissbury Hill to Worthing and the sea.

3 Chanctonbury Ring is an earthwork that dates back to the Bronze Age – pottery dating back to this time has been found on the site aswell as iron age pottery and animal bones. During the Roman occupation it was used as a place of worship by the Romans. It is now chiefly renowned for its crown of tall beeches, that makes it the most prominent landmark on the Downs. Charles Goring brought the seedlings here when he was a boy in the

Plan your walk

Watford
LONDON
Reading
Basingstoke
East
Farnham Grinstead
Petersfield Horsham
Brighton
Portsmouth Eastbourne
Isle of Wight

DISTANCE: 4½ miles (7.25km)

TIME: 3 hours

START/END: TQ145125 Chanctonbury Car park and picnic area

TERRAIN: Strenuous

MAPS:
OS Explorer 121;
OS Landranger 198

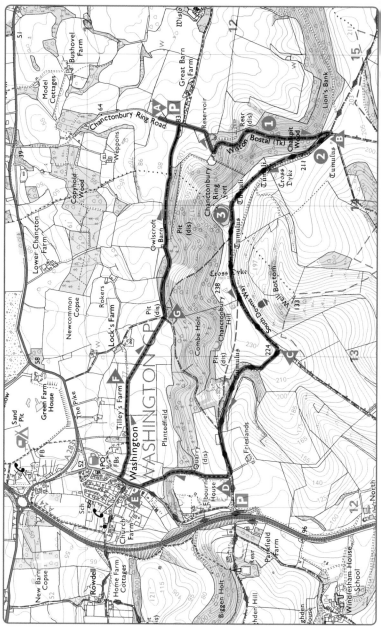

Chanctonbury Ring & Washington

1760s, nurtured them, and lived to see them grow to maturity. Most of the original trees were destroyed in the storms of 1987 although the replanted trees are now restoring the site to its former prominence. To the west, past Chanctonbury Hill and trig point is a dew pond that was built in 1870 and restored in 1970 and is a site of Special Scientific Interest.

C Follow the path to the right indicated as South Downs Way. It goes steeply downhill through trees.

D Walk past Washington Pressure Reducing Station and take the tree-lined footpath on the right marked by a yellow waymark.

E At the road, turn right and after 180yds (166m) take the waymarked footpath on the right just before the Frankland Arms.

F As the line of trees on your left ends, leave the path and head diagonally right across the field to cross a stile in the fence. Then carry on in the same direction towards the far left corner of the field.

G Go through the gate into the wood. Continue in the same direction through the woodland with the fence on your left. Turn left at the road back to the car park.

Chanctonbury Ring

> **66** This popular beauty spot cuts deep into the rolling grassland of the South Downs and is steeped in legend **99**

The Devil's Dyke car park is at the top of the Downs, immediately south of Poynings village. For a short walk this offers a quite astonishing variety: there is some of the best and most spectacular downland scenery, a pleasant stroll across meadows watered by a meandering stream and two delightful villages. It gets its name from the legend that it was dug by the Devil to drown the surrounding land because of the abundance of Christian churches.

Devil's Dyke, Fulking & Poynings

The South Downs escarpment above Fulking

Route instructions

A From the National Trust car park at Devil's Dyke, turn left along the road for 150yds (137m), and then right through the gate marked South Downs Way. After a little while veer right, leaving the main path, to a wooden gate in the fence.

B Go through the gate at the National Trust Fulking Escarpment sign and take the green track down the hill towards Fulking. Ignore any paths leading off uphill.

1 The Downs above Fulking give some idea of what most of the area was like until relatively recently. Everywhere there is soft, springy turf where sheep and cattle graze instead of the fields of crops introduced by modern, mechanized farming. It adds immensely to the pleasure of walking. This is a favourite spot for hang-gliding.

C Stay on the path past the pub garden. Emerge onto a lane and turn left. At the road turn right to Fulking. A short detour can be made to the left to the Shepherd and Dog pub and to see the natural spring.

2 The path emerges in Fulking by the charming and popular pub, the Shepherd and Dog. Just past the pub a spring burbles perpetually out through an ornate ceramic frame. Once, thousands of sheep were brought here to be washed

Plan your walk

DISTANCE: 4½ miles (7.25km)

TIME: 3 hours

START/END: TQ259110 Devil's Dyke National Trust car park

TERRAIN: Moderate; strenuous at the end

MAPS: OS Explorer 122; OS Landranger 198

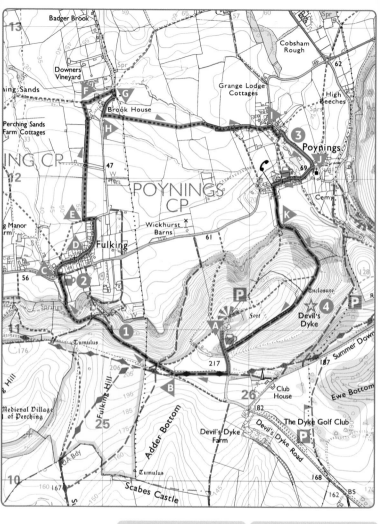

every year. The walk takes you along the main village street, which meanders up the hill past a colourful array of thatched cottages. As you look across to Devil's Dyke, look out for the remains of the track of a mountain railway that can still be seen on the hillside. See 4

D Where the road bends round to the right, take the minor road to the left, signposted Clappers Lane. At the end of the houses, take the footpath to the left.

Devil's Dyke, Fulking & Poynings

E Just before a kissing gate, turn right across a stile. Continue in the same direction across several stiles, past stables to an old iron bridge.

F Cross the bridge, and turn right on to the path beside the stream.

G Turn right along the minor road and follow it around to the right. Cross a stile on your left next to a metal gate into a field.

H Head towards the left corner of the field and cross the stile. Cross fields to a track across a stream and carry on to Poynings.

I Turn right on to the road.

3 Poynings is named after the Poynings family who held the local manor for three centuries in the Middle Ages. The village is quite small, but the importance of the local family is reflected in the fine, cruciform church not unlike that at Alfriston, though it has no steeple on its sturdy, square tower. From here, one has a rather dauntingly clear view of the steep slope rising up to the top of the Devil's Dyke, a view which encourages many walkers to gather strength for the climb at the Royal Oak pub near the church.

J Turn right at the church, keeping to the footpath above the road. Walk past the Royal Oak and take the footpath on the left – Dyke Lane.

K At the edge of the woodland, turn left at the National Trust Devil's Dyke sign. Follow the waymarked path uphill as it swings around to the south side of Devil's Dyke to return to the start.

4 The Devil's Dyke itself is a natural deep valley with precipitous sides, biting deep into the Downs. The promontory formed between the Dyke and the escarpment made it an obvious choice for an Iron Age hill fort, and the ramparts, of earth bank and ditch, can be seen stretching across the neck of the promontory near the car park.

It has been a popular tourist attraction for 200 years, and the first hotel was built here in 1817. In 1879, the landlord decided to boost its popularity by building a mountain railway up the side of the Downs, the track of which can still be seen as a dark streak on the hillside when viewed around Poynings. He also built a cable-car ride across the gorge which must have been great fun.

> ❝ A walk of contrasting scenery – the gentle slopes on the east side of the A273 contrasts with the more strenuous ascent and descent of Wolstonbury Hill ❞

This walk begins at the car park at Clayton windmills. It is reached by turning east off the A273 into Mill Road between Clayton and Pyecombe. This is a pleasant walk with much of interest to see along the way, including the historic windmills and a lofty Iron Age hill fort on Wolstonbury Hill which are such a feature of the Downs.

Jill windmill

Clayton Windmills & Wolstonbury Hill

Trig point on Wolstonbury Hill

Route instructions

1 There are two Clayton windmills, known as 'Jack' and 'Jill'. Jack, the larger of the two, was built in 1876 and is now privately owned. Jill was built in 1821 and has been restored by the Jack and Jill Windmill Society. It is usually open to the public on Sunday afternoons during the summer. It originally stood near Brighton but was moved to its present position around 1850.

Jill is a post mill, in which all the machinery is housed in the 'buck', the wooden housing to which the sails are attached. This whole structure is mounted on a central post, on which it can be pivoted. In its simplest form such a mill could be moved manually, but here,

there is a fantail mounted on the opposite side of the mill from the sails. When the sails face the wind, the fantail is becalmed but, if the wind shifts, it functions like a propeller to drive the mill round to the correct position and keep the sails moving.

Jack has a solid tower and the sails and fantail are mounted on the top as a rotating cap.

A From the car park, turn left and follow the road up the hill. Ignore any paths leading off to the left.

B At the top of the hill, take the right fork of the South Downs Way heading downhill.

Watford
LONDON
Reading
Basingstoke
Farnham
East Grinstead
Petersfield   Horsham
Brighton
Portsmouth   Eastbourne
Isle of Wight

DISTANCE: 4 miles (6.5km)

TIME: 2½ hours

START/END: TQ304135 Clayton Windmills car park

TERRAIN: Moderate

MAPS:
OS Explorer 122;
OS Landranger 198

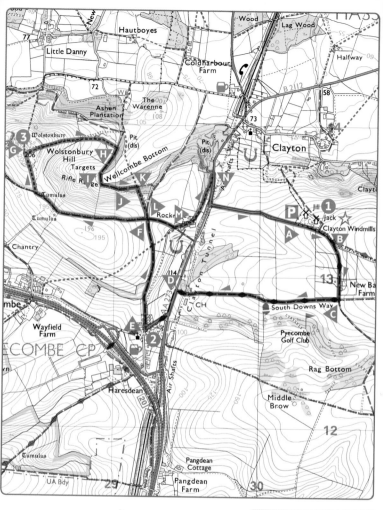

C Just beyond the farm buildings, turn right on to the South Downs Way past the golf course.

D At the main road, cross on to the footpath and turn left. Follow the path into Pyecombe, through the white gates into School Lane.

2 Pyecombe is little more than a hamlet, but it boasts a fine church with Norman arches in the nave and an unusual Norman decorated lead font. The latch of the gate at the entrance to the churchyard is made out of the curved iron top of a shepherd's crook, known

Clayton Windmills & Wolstonbury Hill

as a 'Pyecombe Hook'. It was actually made in the building opposite which was the forge when sheep rearing was the mainstay of the downland economy. It is now a private house.

E At the junction with the tree on the grass triangle, turn right into The Wyshe.

F Walk to where prominent chalk paths cross. Take the second track on the left through the wooden gate. Follow this path, turning right through waymarked posts to the summit of Wolstonbury Hill.

3 The walk up Wolstonbury Hill is especially pleasant, a gentle track that curves round the edge of the bowl of Wellcombe Bottom. There are ditches and ramparts at the summit of Wulfstan's burgh, an Iron Age fort, though they have been disturbed by flint digging. To the east in the valley below is Newtimber Place which used a moat for defence rather than an airy, hilltop site. To the west is the London to Brighton railway line – the return walk takes you over the top of the Clayton tunnel that was opened in 1841. It was the scene of a tragic accident in 1861, when there was an underground collision between two trains in which 23 people were killed.

G From the summit, walk to the edge of the ramparts. Take the path which heads downhill towards a prominent white building on the main road to the left of the woodland.

H Enter the woodland through the gate and immediately turn right on to the bridleway.

I Go through the gate, and follow the path round to the left.

J At the next gate, turn left into the wood. Take the left of the two paths.

K Where a path crosses, turn right up two flights of steps. Emerge from the wood across a stile. Carry straight on to another stile on the left. Cross it and turn right keeping the fence on your right.

L At the footpath crossing, turn left down the hill.

M Turn left at a large clearing and walk through Three Greys Riding School. Cross a stile and head downhill through long grass to another stile on to the busy A273.

N Turn right uphill and walk against the traffic with great care. Turn left into Mill Lane and back to the car park.

> **❝** A short walk to the summit of Mount Caburn with panoramic views and one of the many Iron Age fortresses in the South Downs **❞**

The walk begins in the village of Glynde, which lies to the north of the A27, 3 miles (5km) east of Lewes. It is possible to park opposite the post office, close to the start of the walk.

As soon as you begin the slow, steady climb up through the fields, you become conscious of the great sense of spaciousness and the wide vistas which are the main features of this walk.

View from Mount Caburn

Glynde & Mount Caburn

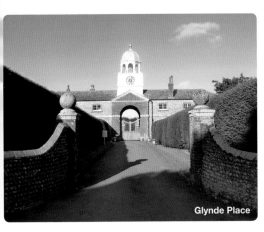

Glynde Place

Route instructions

A Go through the gate opposite and to the left of the post office. Walk uphill through a metal gate. Bear left staying close to the fence on your left. Pass the large area of woodland on your right and head up to the ridge.

B At the top of the ridge, turn left to the summit of Mount Caburn.

1 Mount Caburn is a prominent hill, occupying a strategic site, overlooking the confluence of the Ouse and the Glynde. A farmstead sat on the summit of the hill as long ago as 500BC, but around 150BC it was fortified by a great circular rampart and ditch that surround the whole hilltop area.

This Iron Age fortress was further strengthened by a wooden palisade, but all these efforts proved in vain, for the fort was attacked and overthrown by Roman legions.

The bank and ditch are still prominent features of the hill and, from the hill's summit, you can command magnificent views of all the surrounding countryside.

To the west, lies the town of Lewes, the county town of East Sussex. It was once an important inland port, guarded by its still prominent castle. When the barons of England, led by Simon de Montfort, opposed the dictatorial rule of Henry III, the issue

DISTANCE: 2½ miles (4km)

TIME: 2 hours

START/END: TQ457090 Glynde village

TERRAIN: Moderate

MAPS:
OS Explorer 123;
OS Landranger 198

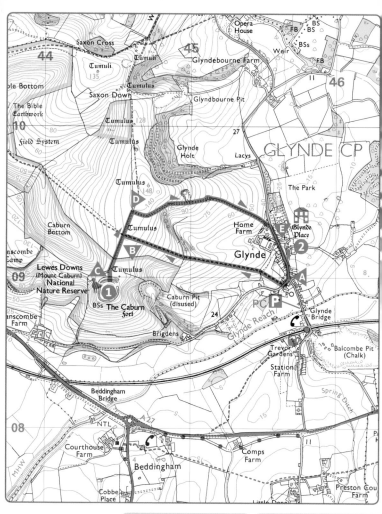

was settled at the Battle of Lewes, and the subsequent treaty paved the way to parliamentary government. The woods and parkland to the north surround the mainly Tudor manor house of Glyndebourne. It was here in 1934 that John Christie established a music festival and then went on to build the opera house that is now world famous.

C Retrace your steps but continue past the original path from Glynde.

D 200yds (180m) past the first Glynde turning,

Glynde & Mount Caburn

turn right on to a vague track by a farm gate and a waymarked post. Cross a stile and head down the tree-lined track.

E At the roadway, turn right passing Glynde Place and the village church on your left and return through the village to your start point.

2 Glynde Place is an attractive 16th century house, much altered in the 18th century, and open to the public on certain days in the summer. It presents a handsome face to the road: the grand entrance through the stable block is flanked by a pair of ferocious wyverns – mythical winged dragons.

The nearby church of St Mary's comes as something of a surprise. It was built in 1765 in the purely classical style that one might expect to find in a London street, but which looks curiously out of place in a Sussex village.

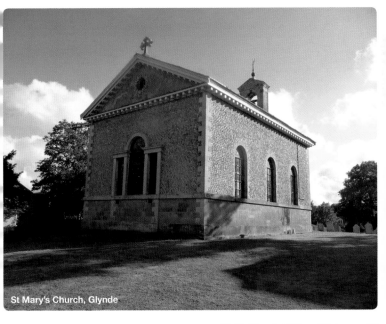

St Mary's Church, Glynde

> **❝** Panoramic views are the rewards for the initial steep climb to join the South Downs Way **❞**

The walk starts at the village of Firle which lies immediately south of the A27 Lewes to Eastbourne road, 4 miles (6.6km) from Lewes. There is a car park just before entering the village next to the Ram Inn. As with many walks in this area that start in the valley bottom, one is immediately faced by a steep climb up the face of the scarp. Once at the top, however, where the South Downs Way is joined, reward for the effort arrives in the form of panoramic views. The landscape offers an intriguing mixture of the natural, the familiar pattern of fields and farms, and the formal parkland of the Firle Place estate.

View from Beddingham Hill

Firle, Firle Beacon & Beddingham Hill

Firle Place

Watford
LONDON
Reading
Basingstoke
Farnham
East Grinstead
Petersfield
Horsham
Brighton
Portsmouth
Eastbourne
Isle of Wight

DISTANCE: 5 miles (8km)

TIME: 3 hours

START/END: TQ469073 Firle village car park

TERRAIN: Moderate; strenuous between points C and D

MAPS:
OS Explorer 123;
OS Landranger 198

Route instructions

A Walk up the village street past the memorial and bear right after Shire House. The church is off to your left. Carry straight on along the footpath with the wooden fence to your left.

1 Firle is dominated by the grand house, which is open to visitors on certain days during the summer. It is worth checking so that the walk can coincide with an open day. Firle Place has been the home of the Gage family since the 15th century but, although the present house has a Tudor core, what we now see is largely the result of a rebuilding in Georgian times.

The surrounding parkland is very much what one would expect from the 18th century, a carefully contrived landscape, dotted with trees and boasting an ornamental lake, in the style of Capability Brown.

The village church of St Peter emphasises the importance of the Gage family to the village. The building itself has seen many changes, but mostly dates from the 14th and 15th centuries. Inside are some superb monumental brasses and tombs, particularly splendid is the Bolney Brass, showing Bartholomew Bolney dressed in armour with his wife, Eleanor, at his side. Of the three Gage tombs, the finest is that to Sir John Gage and his wife, Philippa,

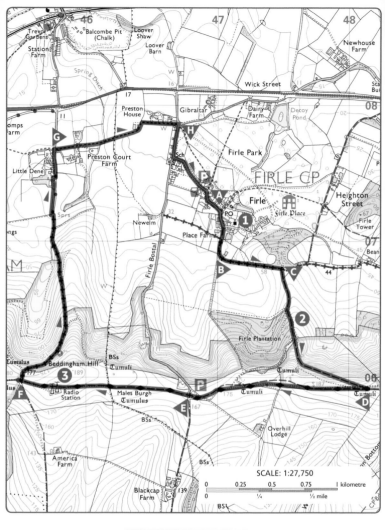

of 1556, the couple being beautifully sculpted in alabaster. The 20th century, too, has brought a note of splendour to the church with a memorial window by the artist, John Piper, installed in 1985.

B Follow the broad track round to the left, with a stone and cement wall on your left.

C At the avenue of trees, turn right through the double gates with the wood

Firle, Firle Beacon & Beddingham Hill

to your right. Follow the path round to the top of the downs following the blue waymarks.

2 Looking back from the steep path that runs up alongside Firle Plantation, you can see a tall tower rising up among the trees to the southeast. This is no medieval fortification but a folly, designed both to enhance the view from Firle Place and to provide visitors with a panorama from its top.

D At the top of the ridge, turn right on to the South Downs Way and walk on towards the prominent radio masts.

E Walk through the car park, across the road and through the gate, still heading towards the radio masts.

3 Beddingham Hill is dominated by the radio station with its tall masts. But there are other points of interest, even if they are not quite so conspicuous. To the east, the top of the escarpment is dotted with tumuli, round barrows used for burials. To the west, set among rough grass and gorse is White Lion Pond, a dew pond, probably constructed in the eighteenth century to provide water for grazing sheep. They are a feature of the Downs and around

this one you can see a rich variety of wild flowers such as harebells and lady's bedstraw.

From here one can see across the Ouse valley, criss-crossed by the straight lines of drainage ditches, to the town of Lewes. To the south, the tall silhouettes of cranes mark where the river reaches the sea at Newhaven. You can also see how people have removed the chalk from the hillside by digging pits, the biggest of which marks the site of the Beddingham cement works closed in the 1970s.

F Walk past the radio masts and, where a gate and cattle grid crosses the South Downs Way, turn right downhill and follow the path that sweeps round to the right. Head down the hill to Little Dene.

G At the end of the houses at a postbox, turn right on to Preston Court. Stay to the right of an old barn and cross a stile to your left. Go through two gates, across a field and past two large barns.

H At the road straight ahead is the entrance to Firle Place. To head back to the car park turn right along the road.

❝ A walk which is steeped in history with a great variety of monuments, ranging from a Stone Age burial mound to a medieval priory and the enigmatic hill figure, the Long Man **❞**

The village of Wilmington, with its many picturesque cottages, lies immediately south of the A27 between Polegate and Lewes. Drive through the village and the car park is just over the bridge on the right. This is a walk that has something to appeal to everyone: it includes a typical section of undulating downland which, unlike the surrounding hills, is not cultivated but is covered by turf and furze. In contrast to this is the flat land of the valley through which the Cuckmere winds its way to the sea.

These two areas offer quite different habitats for wildlife, so that one moves from the high, tuneful call of the skylark rising above the hill to the croaking partridge, strutting unseen among the crops of the lower slopes, and on to find a variety of waterfowl down by the river.

Wilmington & Long Man

Dry valley above the Long Man

Route instructions

A From the car park, go back to the road and cross to the footpath opposite. Follow it alongside the road and then as it bends around to the Long Man.

1 The Long Man of Wilmington is a figure carved into the side of Wilmington Hill, showing the outline of a man, 200ft (60m) tall, arms outstretched, carrying two long spears or wands. He is certainly at least 1000 years old, but the exact age and purpose are unknown. His stance is not unlike that of standard-carrying legionnaires shown on Roman coins but, equally, he also looks rather like a depiction of a Saxon stave-carrying warrior. He is not the only feature of interest

on the hill. As you look up at the Long Man, over to his left near the brow of the hill, you can see humps and hollows which mark the spot where Neolithic or New Stone Age man mined for flints, which were then shaped to make axes, arrowheads, or knives. The long, low mound on the brow of the hill is a long barrow, where the Neolithic dead were buried.

B Go through the gate and at the fence below the Long Man, turn right along the prominent chalk path.

C Where the ways cross, turn left uphill and after 100yds (95m) turn right on to the South Downs Way.

Plan your walk

Watford
LONDON
Reading
Basingstoke
Farnham
East Grinstead
Petersfield
Horsham
Brighton
Portsmouth
Eastbourne
Isle of Wight

DISTANCE: 3¾ miles (6km)

TIME: 2 hours

START/END: TQ544042 Wilmington car park

TERRAIN: Moderate

MAPS:
OS Explorer 123;
OS Landranger 199

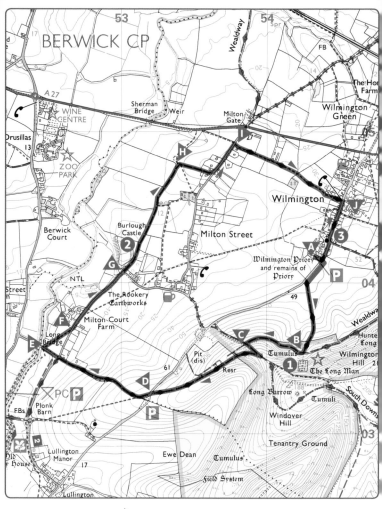

D Cross the road, staying on the South Downs Way, and turn right on to the track. Continue downhill on the path to the road. Follow the road signposted to Alfriston to the river.

E Just before the bridge, turn right on the footpath.

Go through two kissing gates to the road.

F Turn left at the road and look out for The Rookery earthworks on your left (see **2**).

G The road turns sharply to the right. Continue straight

Wilmington & Long Man

on past 'Castlebank' along the sunken path.

2 There is a certain amount of controversy as to whether Burlough Castle is a natural or artificial feature. There certainly was a Norman castle of that name, but the original castle, a simple motte and bailey or mound and courtyard, may have been at another set of earthworks, the Rookery, which you would have passed a short while earlier. The site is in private ownership with no public access.

Carry on along the edge of the field and past a wooden bridge on the right.

H Bear right, carrying on in the same direction along the tree-lined path. Follow the path to the road and turn left.

I Turn right on the grassy track beside the last house and cross four fields. Go through trees on to the road.

J Turn right at the road and return to the car park past the church and priory.

3 The church of St Mary & St Peter was badly damaged by fire in 2002 and the replacement 'Bee & Butterfly' window in the south transept and the 'Millennium Window' in the west wing date from the subsequent restoration.

The yew tree outside the main entrance is thought to be around 1600 years old – it is now supported artificially to see it through its old age.

Wilmington Priory was built shortly after the Norman Conquest, for members of an Order from Grestain in France. It was probably used as an administrative centre for controlling the newly acquired estates in England. Parts of the original medieval building remain as a romantic ruin such as its lovely vaulted entrance porch and mullioned window in the wall of the ruined Great Chamber. Much of the site has been renovated and is available as a holiday home in the care of the Landmark Trust.

Church of St Mary & St Peter, Wilmington

> " A short walk across three of the famous Seven Sisters cliffs that are receding at a rate of 30-40cm each year – enjoy them while they last! "

This route combines a pleasant stroll across typical, rough downland with an exhilarating walk over a section of the Seven Sisters – tall, chalk cliffs near Beachy Head. Turn south off the A259 Seaford to Eastbourne road west of Friston, at the signpost for 'Crowlink, No Through Road' next to the church and carry on to the National Trust car park at the end of the road.

Crowlink & The Seven Sisters

Crowlink village

Route instructions

A From the car park, take the surfaced road that bends downhill to the right.

B At the end of Crowlink village, go through the gate and continue straight on along the bridleway, keeping the fence to your right. Head down the valley to the cliff edge.

C At the edge of the cliffs, turn left onto the South Downs Way and follow the line of the cliffs.

D Leave the cliff edge and go through a gate by a National Trust Crowlink sign. Head down a narrow path and through another gate.

E Turn left on to the path signposted to East Dean.

Pass Seven Sisters Cottage and head straight up Went Hill, through two gates and past a distinctive red-roofed barn.

F Stay close to the trees on your right and head towards the wall in the corner of the field. Ignore the path heading downhill to your right.

G Go through the kissing gate and follow the right hand field boundary to the gate and stile. Cross the stile and then either head along the left hand field edge to the stile at the bottom of the car park. Alternatively you could go straight across the field to the gate and the top end of the car park.

Plan your walk

DISTANCE: 3 miles (4.75km)

TIME: 2 hours

START/END: TV550978 Crowlink National Trust car park

TERRAIN: Moderate; strenuous between points C and D

MAPS: OS Explorer 123; OS Landranger 199

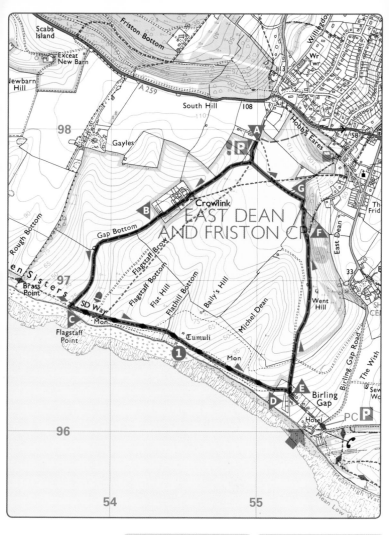

1 These chalk cliffs mark the southern end of the downland. The section between Cuckmere Haven and Birling Gap rises and falls to present a wavelike profile. There are, in fact, eight crests but, presumably because it sounds rather more euphonious, they are always known as the Seven Sisters, and three of them are included on this walk. This is superb scenery with

Crowlink &
The Seven Sisters

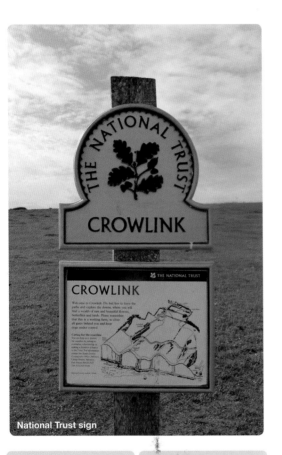

National Trust sign

the cliffs rising more than 200ft (60m) above the sea. Most of the area is in the care of the National Trust. An obelisk marks a gift of land by W.A. Robertson, and a sarsen stone on a plinth records the handing over of the Crowlink valley by Viscount Gage of Firle. These generous gifts have ensured that this part of the coast will not be spoiled.

> **"** A pleasant, open walk around an ancient valley at the eastern extent of the South Downs **"**

An uphill section to start with is followed by a gently undulating walk that includes sections of both the South Downs Way and the Weald Way. It begins at the delightful village of Jevington which is reached by a minor road that turns south off the A22 and passes through Wannock. Drive through Jevington and the car park is on the right, just past the Hungry Monk restaurant.

Rolling Downs countryside around Jevington

Combe Hill & Jevington

Rolling Downs countryside around Jevington

walk

20

Plan your walk

Watford
LONDON
Reading
Basingstoke
Farnham
East Grinstead
Petersfield Horsham
Brighton
Portsmouth Eastbourne
Isle of Wight

DISTANCE: 3 miles (4.75km)

TIME: 2 hours

START/END: TQ563013 Jevington car park

TERRAIN: Moderate

MAPS:
OS Explorer 123;
OS Landranger 199

Route instructions

A From the car park, turn left up the road and right up Eastbourne Lane, signposted South Downs Way.

1 Once clear of the sunken lane that leads up from the village, you can see across the valley to the hillside opposite, where low earth banks divide the land into a number of small fields. These are the so-called 'Celtic' fields, which were cultivated by Iron Age settlers before the Romans came to Britain.

B At the top of the hill, turn left at a waymarked post. The South Downs Way carries straight on.

C Stay on the rutted track through a kissing gate at

the bottom of the car park. Go through another kissing gate with the fence now on your left.

D The path heads downhill to the left and divides. Take the less obvious path close to the fence on the left. Walk past gorse and bramble bushes on your right and cross a stile.

2 If you take a detour to your right at point **D** towards the village of Willingdon, you will see path markers at the top of Butt's Brow that are, in fact, some of the stones from Barclays Bank that was destroyed in a bombing raid on Eastbourne during the Second World War.

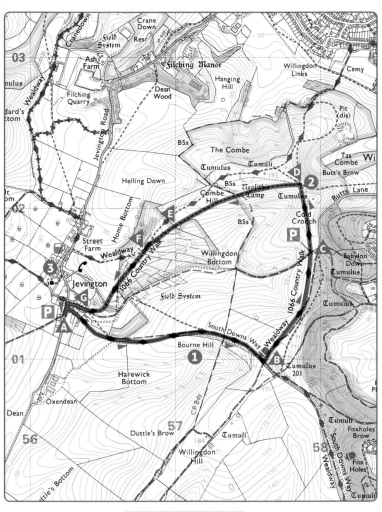

From the top of Babylon Down, there are superb views across Eastbourne to the sea, and back down the deep, shapely valley of Willingdon Bottom to Jevington.

E Head to the right of the small woodland and cross a stile. Carry on straight ahead.

F Walk past a yellow marker post and at a second, 30yds (27m) further on, bear left, staying on the 1066 South Downs Link. Walk downhill through gorse bushes to a kissing gate.

Combe Hill & Jevington

G Follow the road down past the houses and at the main road turn left back to the car park.

3 Jevington village is a charming spot of leafy lanes and pleasant, unostentatious houses. St Andrews Church has a massive, square Saxon tower which is thought to have been used as a refuge at the time of the Viking raids. Inside there is a sculpture of the same period, showing Christ thrusting a sword into the mouth of the Beast.

St Andrews Church, Jevington

View northeast towards Willingdon

Photo credits